Who said it was gonna be easy?

Shoana Cachelle

I'm sharing this book with

_____
(insert name)

Because I believe there are lessons to learn in everyone's story.
Be blessed!

_____
(your name)

I GOT MY FREAKIN DEGREE

he made me touch him

I don't want to do it anymore.

July 1996

A small but cozy space

Something isn't right!

NO

COLLEGE ★ I
DISCOVERING M

* I'm living * with a witch

-I can't

Toxic situation ☐ the

☐ se

forgive me GOD!

☒ Pop

Tomorrow is not promised

4:00pm

May 1990

it's me

☒ AMERICA
☒ ADJUSTING
☒ MISSING HOME

Matters of the Heart

YEAR 1

I think My Parents are dead

Secret Meeting April 1990

* 10 of us living in a small two bedroom house

God Help us!

at 15, I met the love of my life

The Most Challenging Year of My Life!

Adjusting

She slapped the shit out of Me!

* Are we really broke

* Matters of the Heart

① I did the Unthinkable at School Today

Hallelujah

* a good story

16

My

I DON'T WANT TO LOVE AGAIN!!!

June 1990

Roger's chicken every Night

TEEN AGE

SURVIVING

Coming to America.

Looking for a job!

Girl, You Better learn to read *

I filed a restraining order.

looking over my shoulders *

She's Never Seen Black People?!

Is it really over?

The Audacity

30

Marriage Vows

a new start

who did I marry?

DUDE, we share a phone bill...

Did I Just Got STALKED?

A MUCH OLDER MAN!

Sarafina

It was Planned

moving Backwards

— not in front of our daughter

I'm done!

CHEATER LIST.

21

November 1997 *

Unwelcome Home

I saw the light

Grown Up Things

The Nerve.

WORK LIFE

SESSION

It's time for serious boundaries

An Awkward Encounter

Big girl moves

23 My name is Too Ethnic

STREET

Residential Student Apartment

* The bounce Back *

EXPECTATIONS

• YEAR ONE • #1

I Bought A house on my Birthday

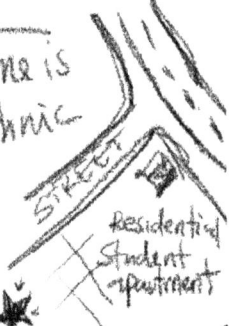

(I cannot believe it)

He hijacked my email.

24

→ Say it aint so →
→ July 2002 — GROWTH

I DID THAT

THE PHONE CALL *TIMES1 *

* I will file another restraining order. He's fired!

The chicken man

No Kissing *

I have nothing to show for it

* Pursuing my Passion instead *

Self-published in the United States By Lulu Press.

Softback ISBN: 979-8-218-03596-9

Printed in the United States of America on acid-free paper

Shoanacachelle.com
Instagram @shoanacachelle
Facebook @shoanacachelle
Twitter @shoanacachelle
LinkedIn @shoanacachelle

First Edition

Cover Photographer: Kofi Dennis
Cover Design: Arthur Togbah
Book Layout & Design: The Kreative Zone - Liberia
Editors: Lorna Samuels
Renae Sigall

This book is dedicated to my children Monahdee, Sarafina, Seylah, Korpo, Derrick, Delvin, and those of you whom I mentor daily!

I've learned so many life lessons throughout my journey, and I hope you can find meaning in these stories that will inspire, heal, and help validate some of the situations you encounter. I love you all very much.

Love, Mom
(Aunty Sho)

I will make sure
to share all my
thoughts in the
pages of this
diary daily.

Preface

My mother gifted me with my first diary when I was ten years old. These diaries and journals have helped me through multiple life changes, including relocation, bullying, love, marriage, miscarriage, obsession, adoption, acceptance, and transformation. The outcome of every story had a powerful lesson to learn. I quickly realized that writing daily entries was a therapeutic tool that helped me overcome many obstacles while navigating through life.

As I grew older, my diaries turned into journals that safely held my most sacred stories. Writing has been healing for me. This book opens up my past in hopes that you will find meaning in each journal entry that will inspire, or transform your life. Some of the names have been changed to protect a few reputations. These entries are honest, authentic, and raw. Yes, they make me vulnerable, but it's all worth it if my vulnerability can inspire and reconstruct just one person's life.

January 16, 2020

Adolescence
It's Me

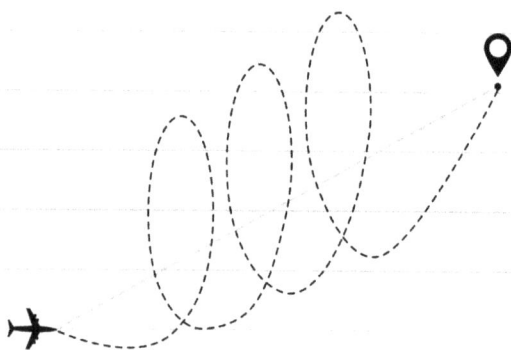

It's
Me

The following diary entries took place during my adolescent years. Growing up was untraditional and challenging, yet filled with love, and discoveries. I'm the middle child; seven years younger than Esther, my older sister, and two years older than Thembi, my youngest. I've always felt like I didn't fit in with our trio so I often found myself alone. However, I was never lonely. My imagination created the perfect world in which I would exist for most of my childhood. As a teen, I was given adult responsibilities earlier than most kids. Looking at it now, it gave me a head start over my peers.

The journey may have been difficult, but who said it was gonna be easy? I don't regret a single lesson learned or experience that I've had.

Secret Meeting

Dear Diary,

It's all over the radio now. Liberia is in the middle of a devastating civil war. Thousands of people are being murdered in the countryside. I heard on the radio that there is an army of rebels that are against the current government. These rebels have their headquarters in Nimba, the county on the border of Liberia and Ivory Coast. According to the news, President Doe wants to bomb the entire County of Nimba. He has given the residents only two weeks to evacuate. Charles Taylor, leader of the rival, stated on BBC radio, if the president bombs Nimba, he will bomb Grand Gedeh, another county in Liberia. I don't know how true that is, but I am terrified!

Some people say that the rebels have magical powers and can physically transform into all types of creatures and objects like snakes, trees, or they can simply disappear. If this is true, we need to start praying harder for protection and that these leaders have compassion for the people of this country.

Mommy went shopping for an entire month's worth of food today. There is a rumor that soon all the markets will close. Liberia has been at war for more than 4 months now. I hope this all ends soon.

****

This evening, my parents had a secret meeting with my aunts, uncles, and grandparents in our living room. They had all the children stay out in the yard. My older sister, Esther, wanted to find out what they were meeting about, so she snuck up next to the window to listen in, but got caught. "Esther, get away from the window", a voice shouted from inside! She came running back to the concerned group of us standing in the middle of the yard. We all had questions. What was happening that was so secretive? About an hour later, the adults exited the house and our cousins were called to their cars. My parents called us into the living room. There was an uncomfortable eerie stillness in the room. They instructed us to each pack one suitcase with our most valuable possessions. We were also told that we would leave for the Ivory Coast in two days with Aunty Eva. Apparently, the war is pretty bad, and the rebels are advancing towards the city. Dad and Mom will pack up and join us in about a week.

I was trying to contain my excitement, as we no longer had to go to school for the rest of the year. We are also about to travel with our closest cousins to a new country we have never visited before. I think I'm going to pretend it's an early birthday trip for my 14th birthday instead of this horrible civil war we are experiencing. But wait, what about our friends? It's Friday, and we will be leaving on Sunday. I can't believe we are leaving without telling them goodbye. I am excited about leaving, but what If I never see my friends again? Wait! What if I never see my boyfriend again? Oh no! What if I never see my home again? This trip is terrible! We are going to a French-speaking country, and I don't even speak French! I'll give you more details soon, but I'm going to bed for now.

Goodnight!
It's Me

I think my parents are dead.

Dear Diary,
We have been here in the Ivory Coast for about a month as refugees waiting for my parents to arrive from Liberia. They promised they would be here soon after we left, and it still has not happened. There are 10 of us living in a small two bedroom house.

*****

Every night I've had to be creative. There are not enough beds for everyone but the floor is cold, dusty, and hard. The softest place to sleep is in my suitcase. Each night, I take out the harder clothing items like my jeans, belts, and shoes. I then curl up perfectly in my large black suitcase and use my jacket as covers to keep me warm and cozy during the night. Every morning, my back aches and my left arm is numb from sleeping on it all night. I can't believe this is our life now.

I'm crying as I write this. I think my parents are dead, but Aunty Eva doesn't want us to know as she tries to figure out what to do with us. Last week, my Aunt and uncle walked into the house and surprised my cousins. We were all so happy to see them. I ran to the door to see if my parents were behind them, but they weren't. I immediately asked if Mommy and Daddy were on their way too, but the look on their faces immediately told the entire story. My uncle said they had lost touch with my parents, but he was sure they would be arriving soon. I didn't believe him. He hesitated as he spoke those words. The news reporter on TV stated no more planes were coming or going to Liberia because it was too dangerous. If my parents aren't dead, they will most likely die. I can't live without them. I just can't! God, please let my parents walk through that door. Wake me up from this nightmare!

It's Me

God Help Us.

Dear Diary,

It's been about ten days since my cousins left with their parents for the States. My heart physically hurts. The pain in my chest is something I have never felt before. I'm not getting enough air right now. I can't breathe!

I've been crying for hours. My eyes are swollen and puffy. My head is throbbing. It has never hurt like this before. I feel like it's about to explode. I don't want to be here. I don't want to be an orphan. I just want my life back. I don't want war. I want peace. I want my mommy and daddy to magically appear, hold me, and tell me that everything will be ok. I want my friends. For the first time in my life, I miss Math and English class. God, please help us! Help Liberia and the leaders that are fighting. What did we do to deserve this? God help us!

It's Me

Hallelujah

DIARY!

Mommy and Daddy walked through the door last night. Oh my God! We were sitting in the living room watching the news like it was my favorite movie. "Hello," said a familiar voice behind us, coming from the kitchen. Was I hearing things? I froze as my brain tried to process the voice of my mother. I immediately experienced a series of emotions from uncertainty, fear, and anxiety to joy, happiness, and peace. It all happened in about ten seconds. "Mommy, Daddy!" we shouted in unison. My legs felt heavy. While my sisters ran to hug them, I was too overwhelmed with emotions and couldn't stand up, so I sat there with my arms outstretched hoping one of them could just lift me off the floor. They did!

I had prayed for this day for over a month. Every single day I asked God to bring Mommy and Daddy to us. I wanted them to walk through that very door. Today he answered my prayers. I love you God, with all my heart.

I have to go now. My parents are about to tell us the story about how they escaped!

It's Me

America

Dear Diary,
Most summers we travel to Philadelphia, Pennsylvania to visit Mommy's family. I still can't believe Mommy is American since she blends into the Liberian setting so well. We usually stay at at my Grandmother's house during our vacations to the US, so when we left Africa in June, we naturally stayed with her when we got to America.

Mommygran is from the old school. She is strict and doesn't take crap from anybody. She wants things done as she says. I get so frustrated at times because many of her rules don't make any sense to me. Yesterday she said we should never close our room doors...even when we are changing. It's her way of knowing that we are doing what we are supposed to be doing I guess.

We still live with her in her duplex in Pennsylvania. I wish we had our own place, though. It's so frustrating here but don't get me wrong; I'm grateful she opened her home to us. I just miss our home in Liberia. We were free and so happy there. Mommy says she is working on getting a place for us very soon.

*****

I prayed today for Liberia, and then I opened up my bible. It landed on Isaiah 1:2-31. The scripture talks about corruption, burning cities, and foreigners who we allowed to take our lands. It states that we have lost focus, turned our backs on God, and are focusing on material things instead. In this scripture, God revealed exactly what is currently happening in Liberia. The scripture also states we will return to a peaceful country one day.

These verses made me cry for almost an hour. God has spoken, and I pray Liberia will receive this prophecy.

PS...I'm still shaking from what I read. I'm not sure what to do with this information.

It's Me

Adjusting

Oh Diary,

I did the unthinkable at school today. I'm not sure if I should be mad at myself for letting someone get to me the way she did, or if I should be proud of standing up for myself.

It was right before gym class today, and all the girls were in the locker room changing. This one girl, the biggest instigator in our class, always finds something negative to point out about me. Whenever I ask someone to rephrase a question or repeat themselves because they might have been speaking too fast or I just didn't understand, I would hear her say something like, "You know she's from Africa, right?" She is constantly laughing at the way I pronounce words. Instead of correcting me, she embarrasses me in front of our classmates by making jokes. She is a bully. I'm so sick and tired of this. I've never been teased because of how I talk or my clothes. Mommy probably sent us to this Christian school because she thought the kids would be more accepting and we could adjust to this country easier. This is certainly not the case for me at all. I hate getting bullied daily. Today, I fixed my problem physically.

*****

I've never been comfortable changing my clothes in front of the other girls, so I am always the last to change in the locker room. They are all wearing actual bras, and I'm still wearing undershirts. I just got a training bra last month along with my period. Mommy says I'm a late bloomer. Anyway, this girl and I were the last two in the locker room, and she did it AGAIN!

One of the other girls shared while she was making out with her boyfriend, he pulled out a trojan. The only trojan I'm aware of is the story about the wooden trojan horse. The Greeks hid in it so they could enter Troy during the Trojan war. After all the girls left, I asked her to explain what trojan meant. "Oh my God, you think a trojan is a horse? You are so stupid!" Then she proceeded to leave the locker room to tell the other girls. Today was the last time ANYONE would laugh at me again.

I grabbed the back of her shirt and stopped her right at the locker room door. As if I was trained in kung fu, I quickly swiped her feet from under her with my left leg. As soon as she hit the ground, like a lion about to rip apart its prey, I jumped on her stomach and began to take deep, slow breaths while looking her dead in the eyes. In an intentionally low but intimidating voice, I said "In Africa, we get rid of people when we don't like them! Don't ever mess with an African again." I slowly released my hold on her throat and stood up over her. She remained on the floor with her hands covering her face. I guess she thought I was about to whip her butt. I didn't. Instead, I went to gym class as if nothing had happened.

PS...she didn't even tell the gym teacher. Maybe we will become friends now that I've earned her respect.

It's Me

Missing Home

Dear Diary,

We have been in America for almost a year now. This has been the most challenging year of my life. Adjusting to a new city, new culture, and new friends is not what I thought it would be. I miss home so much. I hate the cold winters. I miss our warm, beautiful beaches and tall coconut trees. I miss the smell of potato greens and cassava leaf cooking on the neighbor's coal pot. I miss the boy who walks past our gate every afternoon yelling, "small small ting, buy your small small ting!" I miss the long drives from Monrovia to Grand Cape Mount County for a weekend at Lake Piso with my family and friends. Everyone was so happy. Life was so carefree. I'm tired of being teased at school every day. They have said things to me like, "she can't understand; she's from Africa!" I guess they don't think I understand English because of my accent.

*****

I'm so grateful for the movie "Coming to America." It helped me end all the bullying that I've been experiencing lately. When all the girls were in the locker room changing for gym class, I decided to tell them a story. "I have a secret that my father told me never to tell. He is a king in our village, and I am a princess, just like in Coming To America. I used to ride my royal pet elephant to school. We have drivers, nannies, gardeners, and cooks that cater to us daily. My parents wanted me to fit in, so I was forbidden to tell our secret." And just like that, my miserable school life changed. They think I'm rich and started asking me if they could go with me to Liberia when I return. I guess I'm going to be popular now. Thanks, Eddie Murphy!

PS... I don't think I will get teased anymore about wearing my L.A Gears instead of Reeboks. Hopefully, mom will be able to afford to buy me some new purple Reeboks, like Sherita's, for my next birthday.

It's Me

Are We Really Broke?

Dear Diary,

This war is out of hand. I would have never thought that it would have lasted this long. It's been two years now. I pray it will end soon.

In Liberia, we were not wealthy, but we were comfortable. Mommy and daddy worked hard to give us a good life. Almost every year, we went on vacation. In addition to regular school, Daddy sent us to Alliance Francaise, a french school in Congo town. He wanted his daughters to be bilingual. They sent us to dance classes and swimming lessons to be well-rounded. My parents always wanted the best for us.

Today, I heard mommy in the room crying. I went in there to comfort her. I know she has not been happy for a while. My Mother was the accounting manager at the largest Hotel in Liberia, Hotel Africa. She knows her stuff. She lived in Liberia for 14 years after meeting my dad here in America at Lincoln University. Since we have been back in the US, she has worked two or three jobs to keep food on the table. Folks here must feel like African accounting is inferior to American accounting. I know that whoever gives my mother a chance to work in her field will be blessed.

Mommy was crying because she didn't have any money left in her savings. She has to pull us out of private school and dance class. This is happening. We are broke, and it isn't a joke!

****

I wish my sister Esther worked at a restaurant with more food options than at Roy Rogers. We usually wait until 10:30 for her to get home most nights these days with whatever leftover chicken the restaurant didn't sell. Instead of throwing the food out, the manager gives it to employees to take home. I'm grateful to have food, but I'm tired of Roy Rogers chicken every night!

It's Me

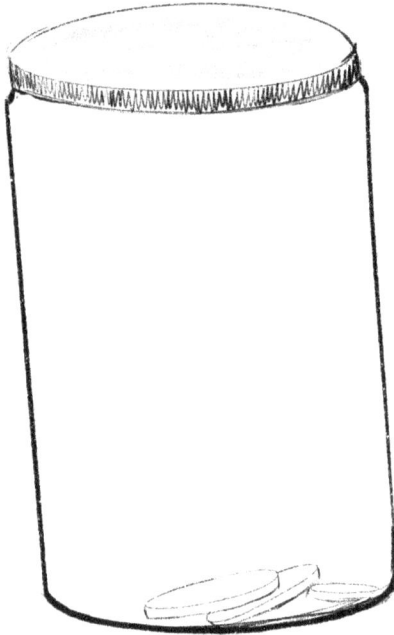

Matters Of The Heart

At 15, I met the love of my life. I attended
a school where most students were white.
I had not seen one African since I moved
into that community in 1990. I remember the
first day I saw Howard like it was yesterday.
He had these incredible hazel green eyes, a
sun-kissed complexion, and medium brown
hair. I would sometimes catch him staring.
The day he winked at me, I knew he would
be mine. He was an athlete, the captain
of the track team, and a basketball team
member. He was 16 and so wise for his age.
Many of the girls seemed to have a crush
on him. I understood, even at 15, that being
authentically me would make me stand out
so that he would notice and approach me
instead. It worked!

We've been inseparable since our magical
connection three years ago. When I'm sad,
he has a way of making it all better. He
is the first person I want to talk to when
I'm excited about something. Even when I'm
upset with him, I would rather sit in silence

by his side. Our love has been so profound, beautiful, and meaningful... until today.

In June, Howard graduated from high school and moved to Maryland with his sister for a part-time job as a lifeguard. It's the first time we have been separated. Recently, I've noticed that he hasn't been answering my calls as he usually does, and he's not calling me as often. I felt like something was wrong. I would have never thought it would have to do with another girl in a million years. He has been faithful, honest, and truthful. He is always extremely honest (sometimes a little too much), but I appreciated that. A jealous girl could never be his girlfriend. You have to be super secure to be in a relationship with him.

I had been trying to reach him for the past two days. I called his sister Sara, but she hesitated when I asked for him. I knew she was covering for him, but I also felt she disapproved of what he was doing based on her response to the question. When he finally returned the call, I asked him where he'd been. He paused and told me he would call me right back. Within two minutes, I heard a knock on my door. It was him. I jumped into his arms with excitement. Was he trying all along to surprise me? I didn't want to let go. It had been an entire summer. When I looked into his eyes, I could see something was bothering him. "Let's go outside and talk," I said. He looked nervous, and I knew that wasn't a good sign.

He began with, "I met a girl at the pool. I was just being nice at first. She came daily and invited me over. That's when she seduced me. My flesh was weak." He began to cry as he begged for my forgiveness. We had a solid Godly relationship. I wanted Howard to be my first. We had planned to wait for marriage. There were a lot of firsts with him, including my first kiss. When he uttered those words today, I felt instant heat overcome me. My heart was immediately shattered into a million pieces. I was broken because I had placed so much trust in one human. He not only broke our bond, but he is tarnished, tainted, and ugly to me right now. I can't breathe. My heart hurts. My hands are shaking as I write. I don't know how to trust him again.

We both sat on the front steps and cried for an hour. It's over! I love him so much, but I hate him even more. I've heard of heartbreaks, but it's numbing the first time it happens. I feel powerless, cheated, and angry. I was overcome with a feeling of revenge and wanted to hurt him more than I've been hurt. I don't think I will ever allow myself to love this way again.

PS: God help me through this ordeal. This pain is something I have never felt in my life. If this is how love treats people, then I don't ever want to be in love again.

She Slapped The Sh*T out of Me.

I'm 18 years old now, and it's time to transition to a journal. Diaries are a thing of the past at my age. Right?

Since I left the Christian Academy in 9th grade, Mom has continued in the spirit of the Christian school rules. "You are not allowed to wear pants to school, only skirts," she always says. It's really not fair. What's wrong with pants, jeans, or shorts? If God didn't want us to wear them, he would not have had man create them. I'm tired of all these stupid rules that make no sense. I've watched my friends confront their parents, and nothing happened. The other day, my friend's mom just stood there and listened while her daughter yelled at her because she was upset. I would never yell at my mom, but I need her to start hearing me since I'm an adult. I realize God has given me a voice, and I need to assert it. Why have I been so scared to speak my mind to Mom about certain situations? She is not God. She is human like me. As a matter of fact, we are like girlfriends.

This morning, I decided to stand my ground and wear pants to school. It's my senior year, and I just bought these super cute red jeans that go with my favorite jacket. I had planned to come downstairs right when it was time to walk out of the door so she wouldn't have time to send me back to change.

She yelled, "Girls, it's time to leave for school!" I ran down the stairs and tried not to make eye contact. "What are you wearing, Shoana?" she asked. "My new pants to match my jacket," I responded. Her look sent chills through my body. I could feel my heart beating harder and faster. "This is the moment to speak boldly," I told myself. "Mom, I'm 18 years old now, and if I want to wear jeans, I should be able to." My head tilted high with pride. She said nothing, I grabbed my car keys and my bookbag from a chair next to the door and walked by my mother. It would've been my last day on earth if looks could kill. "Get back upstairs and change your clothes," she said in a low, quiet voice. It's that voice mom uses to signal the upcoming wrath of fire. I was not the usual obedient child in that instant as I yelled, "No, mom, not today-OUCH!

You slapped me!". She really did slap me right across the cheek. The joy and pride minutes before, instantly converted to pain and suffering. A warm tear rolled down my face. My anger dissolved when I saw a tear roll down her cheek too. "Why would you make me do that to you? What has gotten into you?" Mom regretted slapping me. However, my guilt did not make up for the hurt I caused her. My parents have raised me to be respectful. "Mom, I'm so sorry. Please don't cry. It will never happen again. Please forgive me," I begged.

Surviving

I am furious right now! My friend is having a sleepover with all the senior girls at her house. I just asked daddy if he could take me. Not only did he say I couldn't go, but he served me with "you are not in this country to have fun, we are here to survive." Those words pierced my heart. What does that even mean? It's not my fault these are the cards we have been dealt. I just want to be a typical teenager. This game of life is not fair. I don't want to play it anymore.

****

I'm graduating from high school next week. I'm really excited! I've been asked to be the graduation speaker for the Strath Haven Class of 1995. This has been quite a journey of patience and faith. No matter how difficult life has been, I've still managed to stay on track and graduate with a 3.8 GPA. I've been accepted to 6 of the seven universities I applied to. I'm honestly in a good place right now.

****

When I was 14, I started looking for a job to help my parents out. I knew that money was hard to come by and that we needed it to survive. I was strong, mature, and I knew another income would help. Unfortunately, no one would hire me. At 14, I looked like I was 11. I was skinny, dark, and crispy looking from the African sun; plus my accent could have played a factor in it. I got my work permit at 15 and finally begged the restaurant owner around the corner from my house to give me a job. I told him our story, and he felt sorry for me. I became a waitress that day. He was hard on me! I honestly think he hated women. He always made sexist comments, so I avoided him like the plague. He offered me $2.30/hr plus tips. It was very low, but I quickly learned how to get better tips. In about a month, I had customers requesting me to be their waitress. I was hungry to succeed and willing to work as hard as possible. There were some nights I was bringing home $80-$100 in tips. For a small restaurant, it was unheard of.

Growing up Fast

Although I was doing well on the job, I also remember many Saturday afternoons, looking out of the restaurant window and seeing other teenagers hanging out and having fun in the neighborhood. I envied them. I didn't get to do that. I worked on the weekends instead.

****

On my 16th birthday, I got my driver's license. This was out of necessity. We lived in one of the worst school districts but about eight minutes away was one of the highest-ranking districts in the country. My grandmother had a friend living in that district that was willing to help us out. I would drive my sister and me to her house at about 6 am to prevent anyone in the school district from noticing that we didn't belong. We would park our car in her yard and walk to the corner bus stop to take the school bus. When we got back to her house after school, we would stay there until dark;

then, I would drive us home. Because we had one car, at 9:30 pm, when most kids are preparing for bed, I would go across town to pick up Mom from her second job at Macy's. We would shower and wait for my sister to come home with dinner, which was leftover chicken and biscuits that didn't get sold from that day at the restaurant.

We were not allowed to hang out, so when we did, we savored those moments as if they would never happen again. These past few years have not been easy, but I am thankful that our family is all together. If anything, this war has made us closer than ever before. It also made me grateful to be alive.

PS...I have wondered what part of my journey would be a good story to share with my peers on graduation day.

Reflection 1

Reflecting on my teenage years, I have to give thanks for my strong spiritual foundation and the presence of my parents' guidance in my life. Although we were privileged to escape the war in Liberia, we encountered an emotional war on the other side. Many young people who fled Liberia turned to drugs, sex, and alcohol to deal with the culture shock. Many of us were bullied and tormented daily just for merely existing. I remember regularly daydreaming about being back home in Liberia again, where life would be carefree and happy. My mental health deteriorated dramatically. My teen years were lost as I had to become an adult much earlier than my peers.

There was a powerful lesson in resilience that I took away. We do not know our strength until we are faced with adversities. We are equipped with all that we need to survive traumatic situations. "Girl, power through it" is how I affirmed myself continuously during those early years. It did get better eventually. After I fully accepted my new life and adapted to my surroundings, I could exist in a way that would allow me not just to survive but thrive.

College

DISCOVERING MYSELF

Discovering Me

College was uncharted territory. I'd lived a sheltered life. My parents, especially my father, were quite protective of their girls. I was eager to face the world as an adult on my own. Little did I know, adulting is not as easy as I thought. I was not prepared for how fast my life would change. Many scenarios would have ended differently had I not had a solid spiritual foundation. In college, I discovered who I was, and made decisions based on what I felt was right without my parents input. I matured a lot during those years.

I can't believe this.

I can't believe I'm officially a college student. I'm on the 7th floor of Laplata Hall, an all-girls floor on the College Park campus of the University of Maryland. So this is how freedom feels? My roommate is from Nigeria. We met during a college tour and realized we had so much in common. We both ran track in high school. Most of the track girls are on this floor. I didn't enter the university on a track scholarship because I wanted to get a feel for college before committing. My goal is to try out when the season starts. This new freedom can make a person lose their mind. Thank goodness I'm grounded in my faith.

There are always boys on my floor trying to hook up with all the girls. I honestly think this is the most popular dorm on campus. Some of these girls are nasty, though. This one girl, Lisa, is sleeping with a different guy every night. This morning, I wanted to shower early before the other girls woke up. When I walked into the bathroom, Lisa and some dude were in a shower stall, curtain open, and having sex in a position that I didn't even think was possible!

I had NEVER been so shocked. For about ten seconds, my eyelids seemed to be frozen open. I had never seen two people having sex in real life. I was thoroughly disgusted yet very mesmerized at the same time. "What am I doing? What if they look up and see me watching?" I thought to myself. Immediately, I turned to exit but not before walking directly into the concrete wall behind me. The sound of my shower basket crashing to the floor distracted them.

I heard them quickly close the shower curtain, but two gut-wrenching laughs came from behind it. So while those two were intertwined, the only action I got was a throbbing headache from when my head kissed the wall. As if this was not bad enough, my morning got worse.

****

My room was located at the very end of a long hall. The door was open, and suddenly I heard my name at the other end of the hall. "Shoana, where are you?" said a familiar voice. My first thought was that Lisa was looking to reprimand me for staring at them while in the shower. When I poked my head out of the door, I saw both of them run out of the bathroom and into her room. Behind them was the owner of that familiar voice. It was my mother and both of my Aunts. "Noooo, how did they get up here?" I thought to myself. I just knew Mom would withdraw me from the university after seeing that. Instead, she yelled out to the boy, "does your mama know you are here?" My aunt followed with, "Isn"t this an all-girls floor?"

I was mortified. I quickly ran into the hall to distract them, but that didn"t work. When they got to her dorm room door, they began knocking on it and shouting parenting advice through the door. While they might have thought this was funny, I secretly hoped I was dreaming. I closed my eyes as tightly as I could, and when I opened them, I could still see my family walking toward me, laughing hysterically. This situation was NOT funny at all.

PS: As a person who has never had sex, watching them in the shower today has made me somewhat curious. I wonder if these thoughts are sinful?

I'm living with a witch

So remember how I told you about my wonderful roommate? Just erase that thought. I'm convinced the devil sent her!

Our first month in the dorms was terrific. We shared everything from food, clothes, sheets, and even combs. We were that close. I knew a few guys on campus from either Liberia or high school. They would always come by to hang out in our room. She had her eye on my friend, Cole, and my cousin, Eric. They were always nice to her but were not attracted to her. I knew Cole preferred white girls, but I didn't want to tell her. I laughed each time I saw her flirting with them. I asked Eric one day why he didn't just tell her he wasn't interested, but in response, he stated that he didn't want to hurt her feelings. I wish they would have told her because what happened next might have been avoided.

She decided to confide in me about her feelings for Cole.

I couldn't sit there and pretend, so I shared that both guys were not interested. I tried to phrase it in the nicest way I knew how but she lost it. You would have thought I conjured up an evil spirit. I had flipped a switch, and everything went downhill from there.

The following weekend, my boyfriend came from Pennsylvania. She hardly conversed with him, which made the entire weekend uncomfortable for us both. After he left, she declared, "No boys in our room and your boyfriend can't stay the night either!" She knew this would hurt the most. Hudson and I have been together for the past four years (on & off). He drives down from Pennsylvania one weekend of each month to see me. They have always been cool, so I'm shocked she banned him too. To make matters worse, she has told some lies to the girls on the track team, and now most of them are acting weird towards me. She is literally making my life miserable.

Last night, I came home, and there was a party in our room. I had just returned from a weekend in Philly with my family and my boyfriend. I just wanted some peace and quiet. Everyone could tell by the look on my face when I walked into the room that I was in a mood. Girls were all over my bed. When I asked her to turn the music down, she turned it up even louder. To avoid drama, I exhaled loudly, dropped my bag on my desk, and headed over to Cole's dorm. He calmed me down and walked me back to my dorm hours later. I planned on kicking everyone out but when I entered, the room was empty.

*****

This morning, I woke up to my roommate sneaking milk out of my fridge to eat with her cereal. Not only was she eating my food, but she was wearing my only white blouse too. I never knew I could have this much dislike for one individual I cared for so much.

I went off on her. At this point, it's unhealthy for us to remain in the same room.

I can't deal with toxic situations. I don't trust her, nor can I stand being around her. Mom told me to pray about this. I have, but It's not getting better. I think God wants me to take action. I'm heading to the admission office to request a room change for the second semester. I can't live with this witch anymore.

He made me touch him

Yesterday, I watched an episode of Oprah that shed some serious light on some past trauma that began when I was twelve up until I was about 14. Dr. Phil, a therapist, was a guest on Oprah. He shared with a young lady who had experienced similar trauma, that everything that happened was not her fault. He explained to her how she was manipulated and violated. As she divulged more of her story, I began to cry uncontrollably. The young lady's story mirrored my situation a few years back while I was in Liberia.

Until today, I had locked my secret in an imaginary box and hid the key from everyone, including myself. Hearing this girl's story on TV made me realize that I had to let the secret out so I could heal properly. I thought that if I forgot about it, the feeling of guilt would go away. I was wrong. You can't just sweep this stuff under the rug. It always comes back with a vengeance.

****

So, there was a man my grandmother hired to take care of her home. He had always been a part of our family. He grew up alongside my dad, helped to raise my aunts, and had taken care of our family home as far back as I can remember. Daddy and Mommy even built him a small apartment in our compound two years ago. Little did they know that apartment would be where their daughter would discover adult things. One Saturday afternoon, I knocked on his door and asked to see his new apartment. He invited me in for a tour.

The space was small but cozy. It had a twin bed, a dresser, and an old comfortable chair in the corner. I could tell he was very proud of his new space. I also distinctly remember seeing a Bible on the bedside table. "You like it?" he asked. "It's pretty! I know you're happy for your new place?" I responded. "It has everything I need. I want to show you something," he said softly. He proceeded to lift up his mattress. Under it were lots of magazines. When I looked closer, I noticed that on the cover of each magazine were women in bras and panties. I walked over for a closer look. He handed me a magazine and told me that I could open it. I knew it was wrong but I was 12 years old and curious.

When I opened the first magazine, I was in shock. The models were stark naked and touching themselves in private places. I immediately shut the book and looked at him in horror. The smile on his face convinced me that it was okay and was our little secret. He assured me no one would ever know and anytime I wanted to look at the magazines, he would let me.

Over the months, he invited me into his room a few more times to look at these magazines. One day, he extended his hand to hold mine. I noticed that the top button and zipper on his pants were open. He then took my hand and rubbed it softly on his private area. I was terrified and shaking. He smiled as he moved my hands back and forth over his white underwear. Shortly after, his entire penis was exposed. I had never seen one before. As soon as he pulled his underwear down, it popped out like a jack-in-the-box toy I had as a kid. He took my hand, wrapped it around his entire penis, and guided it up and down slowly. Before I knew it, he had my hand moving faster and faster until his milky, sticky substance was all over my hand. It was disgusting! I quickly jerked my hand away from him. As I began to walk out of his room, he called me, "Shoana, remember this is our little secret!" I left.

He was always very kind. He would make me soup when I was sick and helped me clean when I was doing my chores. I knew what he was making me do with him in private was wrong but I was afraid to tell because I didn't want to get him in trouble. If I told my parents, he would have been arrested and I would have been punished, or so I thought. He made me feel like what he was doing was not bad at all. He was helping to prepare me for adulthood. I believed it because he never hurt me, so I continued to go along with it. He even said I was a fast learner because every time after that day he would give me a compliment. "You are getting better at doing this," he would say.

I didn't want to do it anymore, but he had a way of convincing me. This happened several times for almost 2 years, but today I put an end to it.

****

I walked into my grandmother's house this morning, looking for her. He was in the kitchen washing dishes when I entered. I greeted him and headed to her room. She was not there. As I walked back through the hallway, he cornered me. He gave me "the look." I knew this meant he wanted me to touch him again. I told him I was looking for my grandmother. He confirmed that she had gone out and wouldn't be back for a while. Today was different. The look he gave me actually scared me a bit. He slowly unbuttoned his pants and extended his hand like he usually did. He had me rub him up and down until he began to moan.

I noticed him moving closer to me. This time he reached for me and began to rub between my legs. I froze, but he told me to relax and that he wouldn't hurt me. He slowly pulled down my shorts and underwear and brought his penis towards my vagina. "I'm only going to rub it on you," he stated. I felt paralyzed but was literally shaking.

He began to rub against me harder and harder. His moan became louder. "Can I put it inside small?" he asked. I'm unsure where the strength came from, but I pushed him off me and shouted, "NO!" I pulled my pants up and ran out of the house.

****

After watching that episode of Oprah yesterday, I understand now that he was not a nice person at all. He manipulated me into thinking that he cared when all he wanted was to fulfill his sexual desires. He had exposed me to a life from which most parents try to shelter their children. He was a perverted pedophile and child molester. I was his victim. He was controlling me. I was a child manipulated by a grown man who knew exactly what he was doing.

As I write this, my eyes are filled with tears. I can't believe I allowed that to happen. It's definitely time to unlock the secret. It means I must tell my parents. I do't even know if he is still alive. We lost contact with him in 1990 when the war hit Monrovia. I'm not sure how this will go down, but I have to get this off my chest. I'm going to tell mom first.

PS: I just told mom on a drive to the store. She almost ran off the road.

Philly baby

So much has happened in the last few months but the most significant change is that I've now transferred to Temple University in Philadelphia. My little sister, Thembi, was accepted to Temple this year so she's my new roommate. It's just like it used to be. Thembi and I have shared a room all my life. I remember looking forward to moving away and now I can't wait to share a room with her again. College starts in a few days. I can't believe my baby sister is in college with me.

I ♡ PHILLY

Forgive me, God

I did something today that's really messing me up mentally. So I have been with my boyfriend Howard since I was 15. We broke up for about a year in high school. It took us time to work through the issues and gain trust again but we made it work. I'm now 21. He is absolutely the love of my life, the yin to my yang. We complement each other. I honestly can't see myself with anyone else in my life.

Last week, Howard got the keys to his first apartment near Drexel's campus. It's so convenient because my summer job at Temple's radio station is pretty close. I haven't told my parents that he has his own place. Actually, I told them that I'm staying with a girlfriend in her apartment so I wouldn't have to commute from home to the city this summer. They would kill me if they found out.

It's been amazing experiencing what it's like

living as adults on our own. We vibe so well together. Last night he cooked us dinner. I was responsible for setting the table and creating an ambiance. We lit candles, jazz played on the stereo, and dinner was so delicious. My baby did his thing in the kitchen. We were celebrating his new home... our new home, even if it's just until the end of the summer.

After dinner, he pulled me up from my seat and into his arms as our favorite song played on the stereo. We swayed back and forth like two vines perfectly entangled. Howard has always been romantic and setting the perfect mood is his specialty. I love this man so much that sometimes it physically hurts when I think about what it would be like without him. I'm not sure if that's normal, but I guess this is what true love feels like.

It was a perfect night. We got carried away in the moment. I'm blaming it all on the wine we might or might not have been drinking. The next thing I knew, we were both completely naked and covered in sweat. I had never experienced this level of passion before. We always stopped when things were about to get hot and heavy. But this night was different. It was as if we were possessed and obsessed. Then it happened. I lost my virginity last night. It was not like I thought it would be though. It hurt! It hurt a lot! He was really gentle and caring but it still hurt! I actually felt a tear roll down my face. I've heard it gets easier and more enjoyable the more it happens. I guess time will tell. I had been saving my body for our wedding day. We had even started making plans this year for our future. We both really tried to stop ourselves but that was the first time we were not at risk of our parents coming home.

Now that I'm writing about it, I'm really disappointed in myself. I know better and it seems now all my waiting has been in vain. I have a year of school left. It's really dumb to risk getting pregnant. This morning, I'm going to do the adult thing. I'll ask him to go with me to the health center at school for the morning-after pill. I'll also ask to be put on birth control. Given our current situation, I would be stupid to think that it will not happen again. What sucks is that I can never get it back or say that I am a virgin on my wedding day.

PS: Forgive me, God!

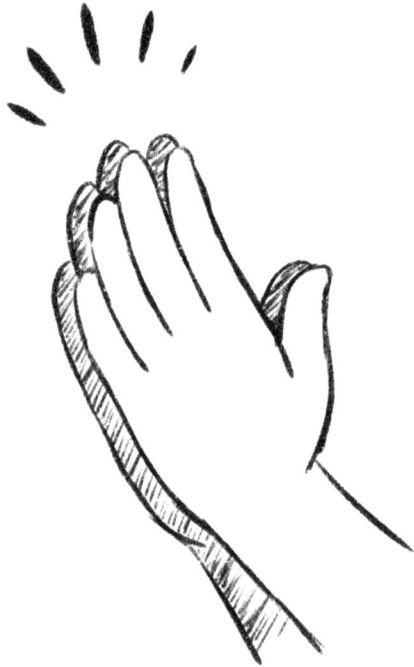

She's never seen black people?

So, it's October and we are finally settling in our dorm room. This year we're in Whitehall, which is a new residence hall and a step up from Johnson Hall, where we were last year. It's actually a suite with two rooms. Thembi and I are in one room, while Brenda and Crystal are in the other. They seem pretty cool but if I had a choice, I would not have chosen to have other roommates. That last roommate situation at the University of Maryland really freaked me out.

Crystal is the only white student in our suite and she has never physically seen a black person. Yeah, you heard me! Looking back on the first day when we arrived, I do remember feeling really weird after watching her parents whisper something to her as they were leaving. She later shared that they wanted her to call them if she felt uncomfortable around us.

Crystal had watched black people on TV. She even admitted to having participated in racist jokes about blacks because she had never seen a black man or woman in person. It's 1997, I never would have thought that in this day and age there would be someone in America who had not seen a black person.

Just the other day, I overheard Crystal tell her roommate she had seen a girl with a bad weave. I guess Brenda had been schooling her on hair. This morning, she asked, "why do black people put oil in their hair while white people wash their hair to get oil out of it?" You just have to love Crystal; she's so naive, yet honest about who she is, and is always willing to learn. I am just happy that God put her in a room with a whole bunch of understanding black women. Instead of getting upset or appalled by her questions, we just educated her ignorance.

Crystal's living in this suite is truly divine. I believe that nothing God does is by coincidence. This should be an interesting year!

Did I just get stalked?

I went to breakfast with my sister Thembi this morning before heading to class in Anderson Hall. I was running late so I left her in line deciding what she wanted to eat. The cafeteria was crowded, and the only seat was next to the window. I never liked sitting next to a window because I get caught up in people watching. The problem is, if anyone spits, picks their nose, or does anything remotely nasty, eating becomes impossible at that moment. I have the weakest stomach in the world.

I sat with my back to the window and began to eat. When I looked up, I immediately noticed a guy about 4 tables over, staring at me. He was tall, dark, clean-cut, and well dressed for a college student. Most people look away when you catch them staring but this guy didn't even blink. The stare was not only intense but highly uncomfortable. It was almost as if his gaze had me hypnotized. I couldn't blink nor could I look away. I don't think I was even breathing at that moment. The sound of my sister pulling out the chair next to me to sit down broke the spell he seemed to have over me. I grabbed her arm as I took a deep breath. She could see I was traumatized. "Shoana, what happened," she asked. When I looked back up, he was gone. I immediately shared what had happened with Thembi. It freaked her out too.

We quickly finished breakfast and headed off to class. She walked to the right and I went left. I was still shaking a bit, but as I walked, I began to pray for my safety. Maybe I was hallucinating. I kept looking around but he was gone. I was distracted by a voice from behind saying, "Hey Shoana... Thinking it was a friend, I turned. "JESUS", I gasped. It was him! Why was he calling me by my name? "It's Shoana Right," he asked? I tried to speak but nothing came out. "You live in Johnson Hall with your sister Thembi in room 611 right?" I could feel my legs shaking at this point. "Don't be scared, I'm not a stalker.

When I see someone I'm interested in, I go above and beyond to find out about them," he explained. My heart was pounding at this point. "Are you serious? If you want to meet someone, this is absolutely the wrong way to go about it," I exclaimed as I bolted in the opposite direction. A familiar phrase I had heard while growing up in Liberia, rang in my head, "foot help the body." "Can I at least get your number so I can meet you the right way," he yelled behind me. At this point, I had made enough distance between us to shout back, "NEVER!" Had I just gotten stalked?

I filed a restraining order.

This past month has been an extremely tough one for me. I've been working at Temple Public Radio for about six months in the newsroom. Because of my school hours, I have to work the late shift a few days a week. The radio station is student lead and my shift supervisor is a senior who walks around as if he owns the place. Honestly, I think he's one of the most arrogant individuals I've ever met.

About a month ago, I had entered the newsroom at about 9 p.m. to write my news story for the newscast the following day. Ameer is responsible for scheduling student reporters and I've noticed a trend. He usually scheduled me on his shift and usually late at night when there are not many people on shift. On that particular night, I was at my news desk alone in the newsroom. He kept trying to start conversations that were not pertaining to my work. I was very uncomfortable and sensed the need to keep my distance. I tried to keep the conversation light but I guess he wanted more. While working in my computer cubby, he came and squeezed himself into the cubby and sat on my desk. I asked Ameer to move and he responded, "you know you want me to sit here and talk to you don't you?" "No, I really don't and you're making me extremely uncomfortable! Please move," I exclaimed. At that point, I was so freaked out. I really don't remember the words that were coming out of his mouth, but I know as he spoke to me, he kept getting closer and closer to my face while I kept moving further and further back. "If you really want me to leave just say it," he stated. "You don't have to leave because I'm leaving," I responded. I got up and exited the newsroom. There was something about him that was intimidating and a bit terrifying. So much so, the following day I reported the incident to the station manager. He was investigated, then immediately fired!

As I was walking to class, I heard my name. When I turned around, it was Ameer. He looked me in the eye as a predator would do to its prey. "So you got me fired? You better watch your back," he stated and then he walked away. Those words penetrated my body like knives stabbing me all over. He terrified me. My eyes welled up with tears. I tried moving but I couldn't. It took me a few minutes to collect myself, turn around, and head straight to the campus police to file a restraining order. I've seen this kinda stuff on TV. I didn't want to be a victim. I had no intention of getting him fired, I just wanted him to stop.

Every single day I look over my shoulders now. I don't go anywhere alone and I certainly don't work the night shift at the radio station anymore. I can't wait to graduate and get the hell out of here.

Girl, you better learn to read.

As a youth growing up in Liberia, I don't recall us being encouraged to read in school or at home for that matter. Here in the US, kids as early as Preschool start reading programs. Throughout High School, I remember using cliff notes to complete projects instead of reading an entire book. I actually disliked reading because it would always put me to sleep. I didn't realize that my lack of reading would hinder my life so much.

In middle and high school, whenever the teacher would start calling out students to read aloud, I remember my heart would skip a beat and sweat would start forming on my hairline. I was super nervous because I never wanted my weakness to be revealed. Thinking back, I'm not sure how I made it through school without being exposed. Little did I know, one day it would come back and haunt me.

*****

When I decided to pursue a career in broadcasting, I clearly wasn't thinking about my reading deficiency. My greatest fear became my reality when I went to inquire about trying out to be the next news anchor at our local TV station. In order to be an anchor on national television, you must be able to read the teleprompter with poise, clarity, and confidence. The funny thing is, this was the first time I actually wanted to turn my deficiency into efficiency.

I had one month until tryouts and I certainly was not going to let this opportunity pass me by. If anyone knows me, they know I'm super competitive. This situation was not going to get the best of me. So for an entire month, I read aloud every text around me. From textbooks, to billboards, to receipts, I read it all aloud over and over again. I watched and absorbed news broadcasts daily. I taught myself how to correctly pronounce words between classes, study sessions, and before bed.

Three weeks ago, I had my audition. I was uncomfortably nervous but I was ready to conquer my fears. I sat in that anchor's chair. Once the lights and cameras came on, I began my audition. Luckily for me, we were given the scripts in advance. Almost at the end of the newscast, they threw in breaking news just to see how we would react if this was the real deal. When I saw what was happening, I almost lost it but then I remembered thinking, I had prepared for this moment for an entire month.

Today, I was offered the position as one of the news anchors on Temple update. If there's anything I took away from this experience, it's that parents have to make reading fun and adventurous for children. This could have been disastrous for me. Instead, I am officially the new TV Anchor for Temple update (our local TV station in Philly), reporter, and vocal coach for Temple Public Radio station.

PS: I'm used to obstacles. All my life it seems like there has been one obstacle after the next, but this one could have certainly been avoided.

Is it really over?

A few days ago, I ended a huge chapter of my life. My boyfriend of seven years is no longer mine. When I reflect on the past year, I realize I was holding on to a relationship that didn't make me happy anymore. He's an incredibly talented and supportive man, but the relationship was not healthy for us anymore. The crazy thing is that I am still madly in love with him. These days, our love feels like strange fruit. I never thought it was possible to love someone so much and still let them go because you know it is the best for both of you.

It started about a year and a half ago when we ran into our friend Cole at the mall. Cole complimented both of us on how wonderful we looked together as his eyes traveled to Howard's neck. "I like your chain man," Cole complimented. "Thanks, Shoana got me this chain. As a matter of fact, she got me this shirt too" and these sneakers. Dag, she just got me a set of speakers for my car!" As they both laughed about all the things that I had gotten Howard, I felt uneasy. I had to stop and analyze my relationship. Why was I constantly showering him with expensive gifts? What was the last present that he had given me? I couldn't remember. I'm sure he would have bought me more, but he couldn't afford it. He worked hard but was always chasing money instead of his passion.

That whole situation with Cole triggered something in me. I started to think about what our future would be like. Would he be able to provide for our future family? I just don't think so based on his current mindset. I had to make a decision. Each month of our relationship this past year had ended with arguments. We are different people heading in different directions. We have outgrown each other for sure.

This year, he dropped out of Drexel University to pursue a career with another multi-level marketing company selling perfumes from his car. You know, that get-rich-quick scheme people warn you to stay away from? Well, he got deeply involved with that company. I'm not sure what those weekly meetings were about, but his mindset shifted after a while and school wasn't as important. After the breakup, I went to see his mother. She supported my decision because she didn't like seeing us unhappy but wished I wouldn't have broken up with him during his finals. I guess I wasn't thinking.

As much as I would love a man who could fully support me financially, it was more important to be with a well-educated man. He dropped out of school, which disappointed me. Honestly, it made me less attracted to him. I had big dreams that didn't include a relationship with a man that couldn't hold down a job for more than a few months. He didn't even realize that his choices made him lose a beautiful relationship.

It's taken me a few days to process all this so I can journal. My heart hurts today. However, I trust I made the right decision.

As I write this, I can barely see through my tears. Seven years is a long time, and I'm not sure how to continue solo. I'm a big girl, and I'm about to make big moves, so it's vital that I find my way on my own.

PS: I pray he finds a woman who can completely accept him. I wish nothing but love and success in his life. Now it's time to focus on mine.

BEST WISHES

A much older man

I broke up with my ex several months ago, and since then, I've only been focused on completing the semester. I honestly have had no time to date given how loaded my schedule is. All I do is go to classes and split the rest of my time between the radio station, TV station, and my shift at QVC TV Network.

Last night, the radio station hosted a happy hour for the staff at Warmdaddy's Restaurant in Philly. It's one of my favorite spots simply because of the grown and sexy ambiance. I usually don't hang out, but since it's my last semester and my favorite restaurant, I decided to let my hair down for the night. While sitting and talking to our business manager, Ciara, a waiter interrupted us to tell me that a gentleman at the end of the bar wanted to buy me a drink. I smiled and declared I didn't drink. "Girl, you'd better take that free drink! Be polite," my colleague snapped. I guess it's harmless to order a coke, I thought.

When the drink arrived, Ciara urged me to go over and thank the gentleman. I was not in the mood, but what the heck. I stood up with my most confident stride and made my way over to his seat. "Hello, I"m Shoana. I appreciate the kind gesture," I said with a smile. Raj and his friend sitting next to him smiled and invited me to sit with them for a moment. I did since everyone at my table was watching me at this point. We talked for almost an hour. Raj really intrigued me. I learned he was an African Studies Professor at Temple and taught at Girard college. I also learned he was a DJ in his spare time. This man is grown and sexy, plus he has his life together...what a breath of fresh air.

Although he was nine years my senior, I found it easy to talk to him. At the end of our conversation, he complimented me for being mature beyond my 22 years. If only he knew how fast I had to grow up, he would understand why I was.

****

The next day at work, I got a call from

Ciara at the front desk. She was covering for the receptionist. She told me to come and pick up a special delivery. When I got to the entrance, a delivery driver was standing there with 2 dozen yellow roses. The card attached read "Hello Beautiful! Call me. From Raj, 215.346.7645." I could feel my cheekbones rising even though I was trying hard to hold back my goofy smile. "You betta call that man Sis, I like him already," Ciara blurted out.

I called. We have a date tonight in Center City Philadelphia.

Hello Beautiful!
Call me.
From Raj,
215.346.7645

Something is not right

I have been dating the mystery man I met in Warmdaddy's for several weeks now. I have never been treated like such a queen before. This man adores me. It hasn't been a year yet since my seven-year relationship ended. I plan to move real slow this time. I have so much growing and healing still to do.

I do, however, have an issue already. I love affectionate and attentive men, but this is on a whole other level. Raj can't keep his hands off me. When we go out, he's either holding my hand, rubbing my back, or stroking my arm. When he tries to stroke my face, I draw the line! I'm sure many women would die for this type of touch but it's ALL THE TIME! Each time I try to discuss any real-life topics he interrupts me with small talk questioning my awareness of my own beauty. This is too much, right? It almost makes me feel like I'm just arm candy. Our conversations no longer stimulate me. I guess I keep comparing him to my ex. We were best friends and could talk about anything and everything. I know I shouldn't compare but...

As if this is not enough, when Raj left to pick up food for us earlier, I decided to do the typical new boyfriend home search. I started and stopped right at his videotape collection. I actually wanted to know if he was one of those men with a porn collection. Instead, I found one VHS tape labeled "update," tucked in a corner of the cabinet. I was curious, so I popped it into the player. To my utmost surprise, there were several newscasts I had done on local TV. The recordings predated our meeting, a minor detail he neglected to share with me.. he had known who I was. Was this all a plan? Was he following me that night? I'm so freaking confused. Why didn't he tell me that he knew who I was?

*****

I didn't ask him about it. I politely put the video tape back and prepared my escape.

When he dropped me off, it was the last time I saw Raj. It was terrible of me to just disappear without an explanation. However, I felt that I needed to protect myself from potential harm. I almost lost my life yesterday in a horrible car accident. Only by the grace of God am I sitting here today writing in this journal.

I was in a really good mood as I headed home from the radio station last night. I jumped into my white Eagle Talon sports coupe, popped in my Lauryn Hill CD and started my 40-minute commute home. I wanted to surprise my parents with the news I had just gotten. I found out that I had been selected as the commencement speaker for my upcoming graduation in May. Words can't even begin to describe how incredibly excited I am to represent my school on commencement day.

Tomorrow is not promised.

I had heard an announcement on the radio right before I got into my car about a water main break along my route but I'm not even sure why I ignored it. I guess I was on a high. I must have been focused on one mission to get home to my parents so I could share the good news.

Everything happened so fast. As soon as I drove up a short incline, I immediately noticed 2 cars were completely stopped in the middle of the 2 lane highway, and both were facing the wrong direction. They were blocking my path and like any young driver, I slammed on my brakes. It was as if I was moving in slow motion on that icy highway. I lost control of the steering and watched my car smash into the 2 cars. The next thing I heard was a bang on my window. I had blacked out for a few minutes and had no idea where I was. There was no sensation in my legs. Unbelievably, my headwrap protected my head from going through the driver side window. The wrap was stuck to the window and still molded to the shape of my head. The sensation began to return in my legs. I looked up but couldn't see through my windshield. The glass was shattered and my hood was smashed in.

I left the accident scene with only bruises on my legs, but my car was completely totaled. My life was spared for a reason. God has plans for me for sure. My car spun around three times, hitting other vehicles, including a concrete median. Tomorrow is definitely not promised. I plan to live each day on purpose for the rest of my life. There is so much I haven't done yet. I know He has big plans for me. It's time to find out what they are!!!!

I got my freaking degree.

This is it! I'm officially done with college. I graduated today with a 3.98 GPA. I not only graduated Magna cum laude but I was also the graduation speaker for the class of 1999. I did it!!!

As I stood on that stage in front of thousands of graduates, I kept thinking about my recent car accident. I thought about how I would have missed such an important day in my life had I not survived. I was given a second chance and I plan to make every bit of time I have on earth meaningful.

I am so grateful for the opportunities and the experiences that I've had throughout the last 4 years. There were many days I felt like I would not or could not go on but I did. College drained me, and at times, defeated me, but I powered through it like a boss. I earned my place on that stage. I feel so accomplished and ready to take on the world. I don't know what God has planned for me, but I know it will require a lot of patience and perseverance. I am grateful for my friends, the experiences, and the journey itself.

When I adjusted my tassel from one side to the other, my future flashed before my eyes. I envisioned myself as a successful news anchor breaking barriers and transforming lives. This is a new and exciting chapter in my life. I can't believe that I got my degree today!

PS: I have my first job interview with ABC network next week!!!

Reflection 2

Growing up, my parents sheltered us. They were protecting us from hurt, harm, and danger. Stepping out on my own during my college years was terrifying yet enlightening at the same time. So many firsts happened.

- Living away from my parents
- Having a roommate from hell
- Buying my first car
- Making love
- Drinking alcohol
- Getting stalked
- Being sexually harrassed
- Ending a 7-year relationship
- Dating a man 9 years older
- Having a one night stand
- In a near-fatal car accident
- I went to my first concert
- Became a professional photographer
- Became a news reporter for radio & TV
- I started my business

During my earlier years, I learned about resilience. Looking back at my college years, I am constantly learning not to shelter my children. Conversations about sexual harassment, and relationships were never a topic of conversation in my parents home. Understanding how to navigate certain situations would have helped me greatly. Today, I have every conceivable conversation imaginable (and unimaginable) with my children. I'm 100% honest and opened to discussing anything and everything to help prepare them for the world we now live in.

Work Life

GROWN UP THINGS

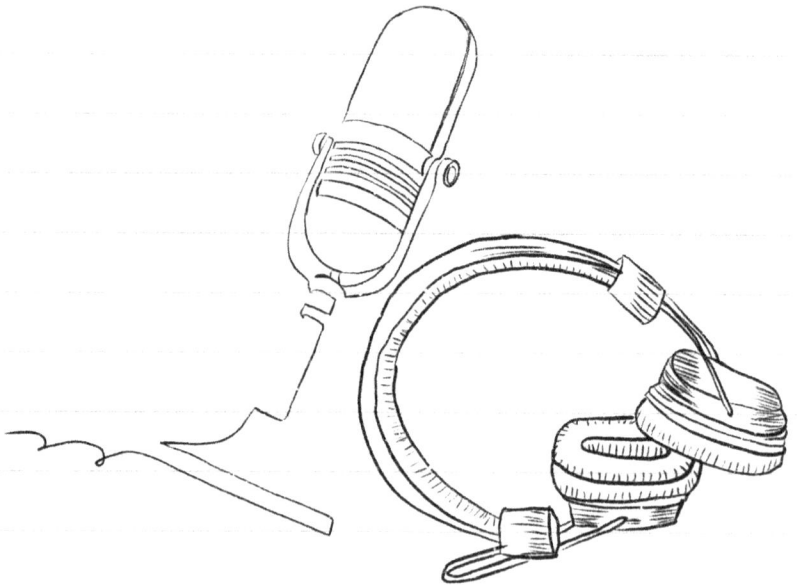

Grown-up Things

I remember wanting so much to complete school so I could be an adult. I felt that going to work was so much easier than having to study for tests and going to classes.

Being grown meant that I could make my own choices. I would have no restrictions, and I could do, and be anything I desired. My parents would have no say over my life. I could be as free as a bird. I thought I was ready, but little did I know how brutal the real world was.

My name is too ethnic?

If this is what it's like in the real world, I WANT NO PARTS OF IT!!! I've played back my meeting this morning over and over in my head. Did this just really happen to me? I am furious, disgusted, devastated, and completely flabbergasted.

You should have seen me! I got dressed in my brand new midnight blue pinstriped Calvin Klein power suite. My meeting with ABC Network was at 9 am. I arrived 20mins earlier, so I decided to say a gratitude prayer and then visualize myself sitting at my news desk. I couldn't believe that I had been offered a job with a major network right out of college. Today was supposed to be the day I signed my contract. Instead, 20 mins after I walked in, I walked out feeling hopeless.

****

The meeting started all well and good until the compliments began. Honestly, I felt they were trying to butter me up. I knew there was something behind all of those compliments. It just didn't feel genuine.

The head of the department started off by saying, "Shoana, you are the best candidate for this job; we are excited to bring you on board; however, we have a few questions for you." The room was so quiet that I could hear myself swallow and what sounded like my heartbeat. She asked if I could use the name Shannon on air instead of Shoana because Shoana (which is my god-given government name) sounded too ethnic. Too Ethnic? All the hairs on the back of my neck stood up as I thought, "Compose yourself, Shoana." I asked her to continue with the next question. She began, "it's about your hair. We love natural hair, but for TV, we would need you to either straighten it or maybe put a wig on during the newscast." She quickly added, "right after the newscast, feel free to snatch it off your head." Apparently, that was meant to be a joke as indicated by her laughter. We all laughed, myself included. The difference was that my laugh was not genuine. I responded, "if these are all your questions, please give me some time to think about it and get back to you either today or tomorrow with my thoughts." They all agreed, and our meeting was wrapped up. I got into my car, and drove away in tears.

I quickly dialed my mother's number. "Mommy, I'm not taking the job," I cried. "What's wrong, Shoana," she asked. I began to explain what had happened to me. I was heartbroken. In this day and age, ABC Network only wanted my face to meet their diversity quota rather than what I could contribute. Their main concern was making their viewers comfortable by changing my hair and my name. Not realizing that by asking this, strips away my culture, authenticity, and ethnicity. I worked extremely hard over the past four years to perfect my craft for this job, and in one meeting, I felt like it was all for nothing. As much as I want and need this job, I'm just not willing to sacrifice my truth for it.

PS: I guess broadcasting is not going to be my future career. My folks are going to be pissed but I will never apply for another broadcasting job. It will either be given to me or I will create it!

The bounce back

Little did I know, but that meeting with ABC months ago was precisely what I needed. It helped me realize that the years I spent preparing were not to work at a major network but to work for myself. I'm not going to lie; I was depressed for probably about a month after that meeting. I felt hopeless, and my dreams were crushed, or so I thought.

I was watching Oprah one day and she was talking about creating your own wealth. The story that she shared was quite similar to mine. If I followed her steps to wealth, my career was bound to have a success story too. I pictured myself being successful. That was it! All I needed to do was picture myself as successful and I liked... no, I loved what I saw. I hate rejection. When it happens, I want that person who rejected me to eat their words. I am now setting out on a path to make them regret rejecting me. I know it's not Christ-like so I'm working on that part! However, I knew that I was destined to be successful and that I should set my sights higher than working for a major organization. I knew I was capable of making them a lot of money with my talent. If I invest that same talent into my own company, the sky's the limit. So that's exactly what I did. I decided to find out what I absolutely loved to do even when I was tired, sad, drained, or unmotivated. The answer that kept coming up was photography.

****

I started taking pictures for theater students around the beginning of last year and I have made some good cash under the table. A few months ago, my mentor, Hugh, helped me incorporate my business. My side hustle is now a legitimate business. The company is called Cachelle Ink. It's a photography and graphic design studio located in Brookhaven, Pennsylvania. TV broadcasting is history. I've always loved photography. I remember taping bedsheets on the wall to take portraits of my friends, and family members. At Temple, I took several photography classes. I remember my professor telling me that I had an eye, so I guess it was time to use that eye to create my wealth. I started this business with all my savings which consisted of 500 US dollars. My parents loaned me an extra 500 dollars and this covered rent and the security deposit for an efficiency (studio) apartment on the campus of the University of Pennsylvania. The studio is now the home of Cachelle Ink Photography and Design.

PS: I hope no one finds out that I'm running a business out of a residential student apartment.

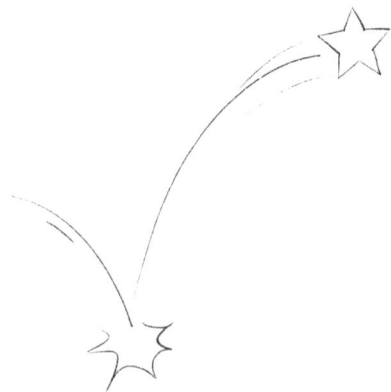

Year one

It's been a year since I started my business. I made a total of $5,000. This might seem small to many business owners but for me, it's money I made independently of anyone. It's the catalyst I need to propel me forward. Next year, I plan to double my income but in the meantime, God has blessed me with something I never thought was possible.

I have gotten frustrated about the parking situation here at the studio. It's causing me to lose customers so I've decided to look for a place outside of the city that would be convenient but this time instead of an apartment, I want a house. I will use the upstairs as my living quarters and the first floor and basement as my business.

I know it will be hard for any bank to give me a loan, but I genuinely believe God wants this for me, so I'm following his lead. I've been looking at many houses, but I just can't afford them, so I've decided to look into foreclosures.

Big girl moves

It's been almost 6 months since I started looking for the perfect home outside of the city to serve as both a photography studio and a home. I've been thinking about growing my wealth and I hear that real estate investment is the way to go. If I purchase a foreclosure and fix it up, I could make a killing when I decide to sell it. I'm young and unmarried so I think I will buy foreclosures, fix them, live in them, sell them and use the money to reinvest in another property. That sounds easy enough right?

After looking for real estate on my own and being unsuccessful in finding the perfect home, I decided to contact Sharice, the realtor who sold my sister her home. She sold my sister her home. I had so many questions and she kept it simple and honest with me. Foreclosures are great but there is a lot of work to make them livable. I'm ready and willing to fix up a space and make it mine.

Yesterday, we saw a property in Chester, PA. It's a beautiful twin home on Ginko lane. It seems perfect! When we walked in, we were hit with what smelled like multiple dead animals. I gasped for air. My dad was with me and he immediately said, "let's go!" Just when I was about to agree, I turned and looked at the neighborhood and pictured my clients being really happy to pull up to a place like this and never have parking struggles again. The neighborhood is beautiful, quiet, and well maintained. I just have to envision what the space would look like after the renovations. I put an offer in. It's my 24th birthday, and I feel optimistic about getting the property. I believe that if it's meant for me then it's mine!

PS: Guess what? My real estate agent just called! I think I got my first home?

I bought a house on my birthday

I cannot believe it! I'm a brand new homeowner at the age of 24. God is my best friend! I'm so emotional right now.

Last year was a good year. I started my business with just $500. It was scary at first as I tried to build up my clientele. The biggest obstacle I faced was my location. The studio was in an apartment building so there were absolutely no walk-ins. Parking around the building was horrendous. I remember my clients complaining about getting there on time but spending about 20 to 30 minutes trying to find parking. Some of them even gave up and left without having their portraits done. I knew that I needed a new location. I honestly think that my income was probably half of what it could have been if I had a better space.

I had to take on a part-time job as a photographer for Portrait World Studio. It's a company that specializes in school portraits in the tri-state area. I'm actually very grateful that I got this job because I've learned so much. If I were to give anyone advice, it would be to become an apprentice or get a job in the field that they're pursuing for a certain length of time in order to learn everything they can about that business so they can apply it to their own business. Working with Portrait World helped me understand the business of Photography.

Whenever we are done shooting for the day, we have to report our film to the office. I made friends with all the office staff as well as the production staff so I could hang out with them behind the scenes to learn everything I possibly could. I helped with logging images, printing, filling out paperwork, and contacting schools. I did basically anything I could do to learn the business. This was not part of my job so I didn't get paid for any of it. I was constantly collecting any paperwork they sent out to schools. I took it to my office and studied it to understand how they market and promote their company. One of the things I did find out was that they never deal with schools that have 200 or fewer students because there was not enough money in it for them. This is where I realized I could make my money. There are many small daycares and preschools in my area that have under 200 students. I'm on it!

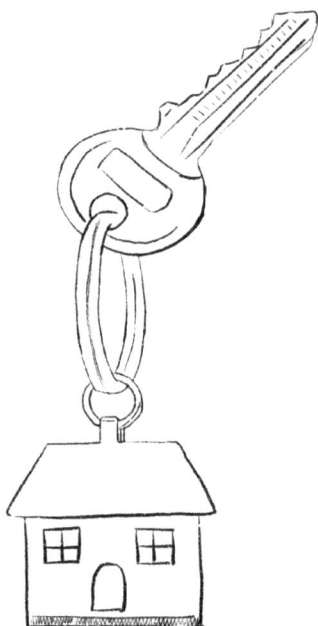

An awkward encounter

He had driven up from North Carolina to Philadelphia for the St. Patrick's and St. Theresa's Convent reunion last year in Philly. I remember clearly, I was at the Greek picnic with Mark when the phone rang. My older sister Esther urged me to leave the picnic and come home because an old neighbor wanted to get together with us. "Are you asking me to leave my boyfriend and the Greek Picnic to come to your house to meet an old neighbor that I don't even remember," I ask? "Shoana, just come to my house, menh! This boy drove up from North Carolina and wants to see all three of us before he drives back today," she begged. "I'll see what I can do, but you're ruining my day," I exclaimed!

After about an hour, I decided my family came first, so I left this fabulous picnic where all the beautiful black fraternity and sorority brothers and sisters were, to go and meet someone I had never seen before or couldn't remember meeting. "This better be worth my while," I thought to myself.

When I walked into my sister's house two hours later, this perfectly dark-complected brother, about 5'8"-5'9", literally flew out of his chair to hug me. "Hi, Shoana! It's been a long time," he said. I had no idea who this man was hugging me so tight. Even my breast got uncomfortable. I didn't want to seem unfriendly, so I smiled and responded, "likewise." All I could think was that Esther made me rush home to see this guy? I was not attracted to him, but he gave me some serious energy. His stare felt a bit uncomfortable. He mentioned that he was about to leave the state to head back to North Carolina and had remembered that we lived in Philly, so he wanted to stop by and say hi.

Before he left, Esther insisted that we exchanged numbers. I honestly couldn't understand why she was so interested in connecting the two of us but come to find out, he had expressed an interest in me and she thought it was her duty and obligation to make sure that we stayed connected.

Say it ain't so.

Who would have thought it would only take nine months for this man to knock me off my feet? I am engaged and getting married! Nine months after meeting him, I agreed to become his wife. What just happened? I am head over heels in love from my core. He is absolutely everything that I've dreamt about, everything that I've desired, and everything I've ever wanted in a man. The fact that he's Liberian is just absolutely freaking amazing! I'm finally going to get my Liberian last name. When I tell people I'm West African with a name like Shoana Clarke, they give me a look of disbelief, but now with his name, there will be no questions about my heritage.

****

Last weekend, I was in North Carolina visiting him. I was so pissed because there was no one to pick me up when I arrived. I tried calling him, but he wasn't answering. I sat at the airport for what seemed like hours, and finally, I saw him jogging towards me in baggage claim with this great big smile on his face, and his roommate was prancing behind him with the same old goofy smile on his face. "Why are they smiling," I thought to myself. "I am so pissed right now, and they better not give me some lame excuse." When he got to me, he started to apologize, and I remember turning my back on him because I was so frustrated and scared in the airport all alone. I was the last person in the baggage claim area. After picking up my bag, he was on one knee, and his friend was videotaping us when I turned back around. At first, I was confused and had no idea what was happening. Actually, I thought he was begging me to forgive him for being late. Instead, it was an honest-to-god marriage proposal with the largest 18ct Liberian gold ring I have ever seen. It looked massive on my skinny fingers, but who cares. I'll just get a ring guard. An older couple was walking past us, and they started to clap, stare, and urge me to say yes. They definitely didn't have to encourage me. I wanted to marry him! I want to be his wife!

What I love about him is how aware he is of our culture. I had grown up in Brookhaven, Pennsylvania, in a predominantly white school. I was one of two Africans in my school. When I went to college, I interacted with more people of color, but I've always secretly yearned to go back home and embrace my cultural heritage. It was stolen from me by the war. Meeting him took me back to my roots. I'm free with him. I can talk about our country's dishes, and he understands what I'm talking about.

The most impressive part of our relationship has been that he writes me actual love letters. He lives in North Carolina, and I live in Pennsylvania. We decided that we were going to mail letters to each other. I receive a letter a week from him and respond just the same. Our letters are honest, intimate, and pure. He knows exactly what to say and how to say it. He's such a flirt too. When he laughs, it's from his soul. When he speaks, he's so intelligent and such an intellectual. He's four years older than I am, and I appreciate his level of maturity. I'm constantly learning so much when I'm with him. God bless our union. May it be pure, honest, and make it last forever.

Growth

So I decided that after I got my taxes back this year, I was going to quit my job at Portrait World and focus all my energy on building Cachelle Ink.

It's been a month since I quit. I'm very nervous about this but I'm ready and feel very prepared to step out on faith. I think this is it! I'm never going to apply for another job to supplement my income again. I did, however, tell Portrait World that I was leaving to attend grad school. It was a lie, but I didn't want them to be upset with me. I was the one photographer that they were grooming for management. I had been used as an example for all the new staff because of my commitment to the job. I also needed to ensure that if it didn't work out I would be welcomed back to my old job.

*****

I reached out to the local daycares within a 10-mile radius of my office, and now I have four schools as clients and two more pending a decision. It looks like this will become my primary source of income this year. I've already made a whopping $10,500. That is double my income from last year, and it's only July.

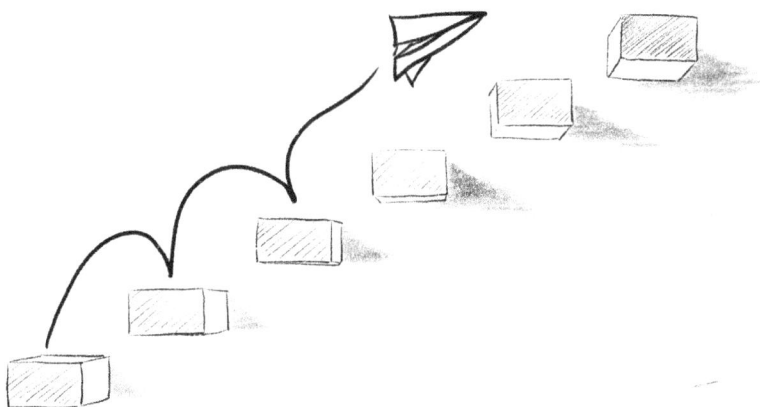

Expectations

Since our wedding day, it's mostly been beautiful. Like any couple, we have had a few issues. My biggest issue with my husband is that he no longer comes into the kitchen to assist me while I cook. When we dated, cooking was special to us. We truly built a unique bond by making dishes together.

Growing up, I never liked cooking, primarily because I was never taught how to cook. We had to learn by trial and error out of necessity. I was terrible at it. I guess it remained that way until I met him. While teaching me how to make Liberian dishes, he actually made the experience of cooking amazingly fun. I looked forward to making meals with my husband.

It's been four months since the wedding, and I'm seeing changes. They are minor, but changes nonetheless. The other day, I asked why he no longer wanted to be in the kitchen with me, even if just to keep me company. He responded with something that sounded like, "the kitchen is your place now!" I was not only shocked but very disturbed by this comment. At first, I thought it was a joke, but he absolutely was not interested in preparing meals with me as the weeks went by. When he does cook, he rather cook alone.

I know this is not a huge issue, but I'm beginning to see someone very different from the man I fell in love with. The other day, when we were disagreeing, he told me that I needed to learn to respect my elders. He is four years older, but that's something you say to a child, not your wife.

PS: Lord, help me. The attitude changes need to stop now.

The phone call

I received a phone call this morning from my best friend, Tinesi. She had just met a girl named Fatima. When Fatima found out that we were best friends, she shared that she had gone to a party with my husband last night. "My husband," I asked? Why was this woman telling my friend this?

Tinesi called to warn my husband that this girl was spreading stories about him and he needed to contact Fatima to rectify the situation. But wait! "Why would Fatima make up such a story if it didn't happen," I thought to myself. I immediately hung up with Tinesi and called my husband. I explained the story to him. He denied it and responded, "I know Fatima, and she was at the party. As a matter of fact, we can call her, and you can ask her if we went to a party together."

That was not the intention of this phone call, but I agreed since he suggested it. "Sure, we'll call her when you get home," I answered.

We both hung up, but I was pissed. My intuition had kicked in, and something was not right. This intuition of mine has never steered me wrong.

When he got home, we called Fatima. She first asked if I was on the line when she answered the phone. He responded, "Yes, she is." She proceeded to disrespect me by saying to him, "If you were my husband, I would never put you through such an incredibly embarrassing situation. Your wife needs to be more secure in her marriage and trust her husband," she stated. I did not respond. I guess I was too shocked that my husband didn't say a word in my defense, considering it was his idea. Fatima answered the question, "no, we did not go to the party together! I met him at the party." He thanked her for confirming and hung up.

I was thoroughly embarrassed. She had accomplished what she intended to do; making me feel even more insecure and regretful. He stood up in anger and began to walk away. "What have I done?" I thought to myself. I extended my hand to apologize to him. When I touched his arm, he jerked it away and proceeded to walk out of the house. I went yelling apologies behind him, but he stormed out angrily and slammed the door. I dropped to the floor in tears. Two days before, I had just found out that I was pregnant with our first child. I should be happy instead of sitting here in tears, right?

I turned to Tinesi for comfort. While explaining what just happened, Fatima called on the other line. "Shoana, you will not believe who is calling on my other line," she exclaimed. "Hang up, and let's call her back on 3-way. I need to hear what she has to say to you for myself," I suggested. We made the call, and I put my phone on mute. Fatima explained to Tinesi how my husband had called her up and asked her to lie to me so it would not destroy his marriage. Tinesi responded, "how do I know

that you're not making this up, Fatima?"
She laughed and mentioned that she had
picked him up from his brother's house. She
even described the details in the entryway,
including how our wedding picture was on
the table near the doorway. His brother's
house is where he stayed this past weekend
when he went to Maryland. I immediately
knew she was telling the truth because she
would have never known about our pictures
on their table by their front door.

Why would he lie to me? Why would he go
to this extreme of calling her and having
her lie to me? What was he trying to hide?
How could he do this to me? Did he sleep
with her? Is this why he was hiding it?
He could have simply said my friend and I
went to this party, and I would have never
thought anything of it. I'm hurt, embarrassed,
and confused. I am even too embarrassed
to tell Tinesi that Fatima was telling the
truth. When we hung up, I told Tinesi that
Fatima was a desperate girl looking to ruin

someone's marriage and that I still didn't believe her, even though I now knew the truth.

When my husband walked back into the house a few hours later, I was furious but decided to do a bit of reverse psychology instead. I began with, "I'm extremely sorry for not trusting you. You have never lied to me before. When Fatima told Tinesi that she picked you up and even mentioned our picture in the entryway of your brother's house, it was hard not to believe her." He immediately took a deep breath, sat me down, and started the conversation with a disclaimer. "What I'm about to tell you may change our relationship forever! I just lied to you, Shoana! She did come to the house and pick me up, but that was it!" he explained. "Why did you go through all of this by having her lie to me when you could have simply told me what you're telling me now?" I asked. He stated that he was scared but he knew the truth was better than lying. He dated her when he was younger, but she was too free with her body. He even went to this party with her to prove to himself that he was strong enough to avoid temptation. He was proud of himself. He had succeeded because nothing happened with her, and all he could think about was me.

Yeah right! I call bullshit!!! How old does he think I am? Why would anyone put themselves through that kind of temptation to prove something? That alone has to be a sin!

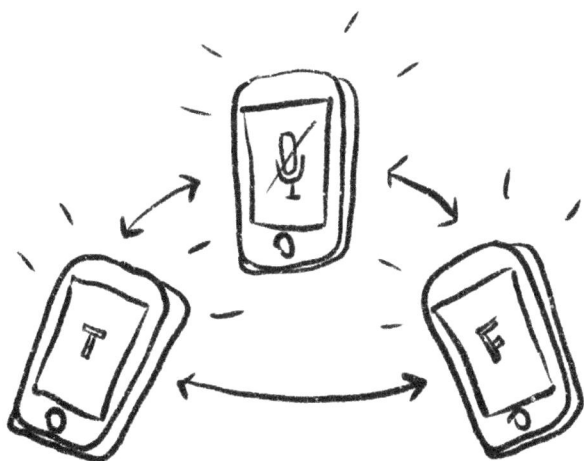

I did that!

It's been a few years since I've written. So much has happened since then. I've gotten married to an amazing man. When we met, he was still in his junior year of college and I had just graduated and was starting my business. We began as a long-distance relationship, but he moved to Philly and into my home when he graduated. He had been assisting me with mortgage payments for the past year, so it felt like the house was also his. It was a whirlwind relationship, and together we created a beautiful baby girl named Monahdee Anaya.

I have moved my business to a proper photography studio. It's about 3 minutes away from our current home. It's my dream location; an old warehouse converted into studio space. It's the perfect artist studio. I painted the walls canary yellow. The carpet is red. The furniture has so much character. The space is simply wonderful. My clientele has doubled, and honestly, I think it's because of this new location. Anyone that walks in refers us to their friends. I now have an entire staff, including a receptionist, a business manager, and ten photographers. Who would have thought in 1999 when I was sitting in my car after a depressing and discouraging contract meeting, I would be here as a legitimate business owner today.

I am no longer self-employed. I am the boss. I have a team of 13 employees in the United States of America. How freaking crazy is that?

YESS...!

Obsession

Okay, I'm officially freaked out by this. I hired Ricky, a new assistant, about six months ago. I met him in a pizza shop. It was on a day my husband and I got into a horrible fight, and I needed to blow off some steam. He came over to the table from behind the counter and asked me what was wrong. He was attentive, kind, and he listened. I needed someone to listen. We started talking about my business, and he shared that he was interested in graphics. I told him I was hiring. Ricky applied for the job, and because of his zeal and passion, I offered the job to him.

Over the next few months, we spent many hours together working to build my company. Ricky was my assistant, so I often asked him to help me pick up my daughter from daycare down the hall in the same building and bring her back to the studio. While I worked, Ricky would play with her and keep her occupied. He was God-sent, or so I thought. He showed interest in designing, so I taught him how to design and create on the computer; never thinking that this man had alterior motives.

Last week, my husband traveled to Greece for the 2004 Summer Olympics, and I noticed that Ricky became extra attentive and extra helpful. He mentioned that my husband was gone, and he knew I needed help. He even offered to babysit, and I respectfully declined his offer. I don't allow men around my daughter alone.

My cousin Eric came over to visit today. When I opened the door, he gave me a mixtape left on my car's windshield. Written on it was my name and the word "LISTEN." The only person I knew who's into mixtapes was my assistant. I was very positive that it was his handwriting too. All the tracks were love songs. "What the heck?" I exclaimed.

Ricky was about ten years younger than me. He was a white male, approximately 5'9", slim with a deep voice. He lived in Chester, and it was evident that he grew up in a black community. The only thing white about him was the color of his skin. He was a pretty decent hip-hop artist and very much into his craft. The songs on the tape were all his. Ricky was an intelligent kid but came from a dysfunctional family. His dad was an alcoholic, and his mom was not in the picture. It's in my nature to help people, but it seems like this boy took my kindness the wrong way.

Now that I'm thinking about it, I remember when I hired Brian, a new intern. He and Ricky were about the same age, but the intern was a student from Temple interested in graphic design. We didn't have an extra desk for him, so I purchased a small portable desk and set it up right outside my door. When I came in the following day, Ricky had moved Brian's desk a couple of doors down the hall. Another instance was while I was in the middle of a product shoot with a male client. He was clearly uncomfortable with the fact that we were laughing. He walked right over to us, sweating profusely, and boldly told me that it was time to wrap up my shoot. I immediately asked him why he looked so disturbed, and he replied that he was not feeling well. Little did he know that my client was gay and not interested in me.

PS: It's time to set some serious boundaries. He is excellent at his job, but I might have to let him go.

He hijacked my email.

That's it! I am entirely blown away. I walked into my office this morning and noticed something awkward about how my chair was left. I'm not that particular, but I know this is not how I left my office. The papers on my desk had been packed into a neat pile, and all my pens were put back in the holder. "Someone has been in here." I had a suspicion about who it was, but why?

The first thing I usually do in the morning is check my email. When I sat at my desk, my email had been logged out, and I never log out of my email (which I probably should). Something told me to check my sent messages. I don't know what it was, but I'm just going to trust that it was God trying to alert me. When I checked my sent message bin, I saw a message sent to my husband at 10 p.m. last night. I opened the email, and it was an email from Ricky. I was horrified as I read the mail. He began the email by explaining to my husband how our friendship had grown over the months. He stated how he has not only fallen in love with me but loves my daughter as his own too. He said that he had to get this off his chest and face whatever consequences that came with it. He suggested a meeting with my husband so they could talk about his feelings. He also said, "I know this is a lot, and If you want to hit me, I'll take it like a man, but I can't change the way I feel about your wife."

As I completed reading the email, my entire body became numb. I was speechless, and my heart was pounding. What was this man trying to do? Was he trying to end my marriage? Was he trying to plant the seed of doubt in my husband's mind? Was he trying to make my husband feel like we were having an affair? This is the stuff that just happens in the movies. It sounded like a plot to kill my husband without me knowing. Those movies usually end in death I wasn't prepared for that today.

I had to get to my husband's office before he opened the email, so I grabbed my keys and sprinted to my car. I didn't call first; my priority was getting there. I called him to come downstairs so I could explain. I hadn't shared with him all the drama going on in the past with Ricky. I thought I had it all under control. I've had several talks and mediations with a third party regarding his feelings towards me. This has just gotten out of hand now.

When my husband got into the car, I explained everything from the beginning leading up to today. He calmly asked, "did you have sex with him?" I couldn't believe my ears. I had just explained my situation, and this was his first response? In hindsight, I blame myself. I should have told him when it started instead of letting it get this far. Lesson learned!

PS: Will I have to file another restraining order? He's fired!

The chicken man

Today might have been one of the scariest days of my life. I pulled into the parking lot of my office, walked up the stairs, and met Kenya, my business manager, in the hallway. As we approached the office door, she noticed a plastic bag with some items hanging on the door handle. "What is that?" I asked. She reached for the bag, opened it, and saw a raw frozen chicken. We were both completely perplexed, but we giggled about what that could be and what it was for.

When I walked into my office, the phone rang. Kenya picked it up, and it was for me. When I answered the phone, it was a maintenance guy that had worked in the building. I hadn't seen him for weeks, but he asked, "did you get my gift?" "What gift?" I replied. "The chicken I left at your door," he answered. When I asked why he left chicken at my door, he explained that the chicken was for dinner because he knew that I liked chicken. He was interested in having dinner with me, so he felt that if he left the chicken, I would prepare it for both of us.

We had only had conversations about the maintenance of my office. The building manager hired him as one of the on-call maintenance crews. Milton was a middle-aged white male who seemed to be nice. I would have never thought anything strange about him before this phone call.

I asked him not to call or leave any presents for me at my door again and immediately called the building manager to report the incident.

A few hours later, the building manager walked into my office to explain that Milton was on medication and had been taken off his meds. He had also had strange conversations with other employees and business owners in the building. They had him removed from the premises. I was told that if I did see him, to walk away and lock my office door quickly. I remember calling my husband to tell him about what happened. It freaked him out. When I got home, he showed me a black box with a very sexy black handgun in it. He told me that this was one stalker too many.

PS: We went to the shooting range today. It's official...I hate guns!

No kissing!

I was sitting in the cold bathroom on the floor, bawling my eyes out. I can't even begin to comprehend what just happened to me. I was supposed to take my little girl trick-or-treating, but I've asked my husband to handle that because I just don't have it in me tonight to do anything.

This morning, I received a phone call from a potential client from Liberia, letting me know that he had landed in Philadelphia for business. Arnold owned the two-story building in which I had my first office in Liberia. He is wealthy and has lots of companies. I see the potential to create a professional relationship, especially since I have decided to take my business global.

With my skills in marketing, I knew he would benefit from my services, so I suggested that we meet. I was impressed with how he had businesses in multiple countries, so I wanted to find out his business strategies. I had so many questions and decided to conduct an in-depth interview with him. There were a few meetings on my schedule today, so I suggested a dinner meeting.

I had worn jeans and a t-shirt to work, but decided to run home and put on a business suit instead. I grabbed my portfolio and headed to his hotel. Arnold suggested that I come up to his room when I arrived because he was finishing up something. I responded, "It's ok; I can wait down here for you!" He insisted that I come upstairs. I hesitated initially, then justified it because he was not in a regular hotel room but a suite, which meant that there was a living room area and not just a room with a bed. I also thought about how getting profitable contracts from his many businesses could be the boost my company needed.

When I got upstairs, he was sitting on the couch. I proceeded to sit at the table opposite him, which was next to the door. I thought Arnold might have been finishing up a meeting, but instead, he was busy watching a boxing match. "Is he for real?" I thought to myself. I immediately said, "Okay, go ahead and finish your match and I'll be downstairs on a call." Once he realized I meant what I said, he decided to get up and leave with me.

We made it through dinner and my thousands of interview questions. He was very polite, honest, and willing to share all his insights and strategies for doing business in Liberia. I was highly grateful for this. When I reached over to grab my portfolio to show him the work that we were capable of doing for his company, it was then that I realized I had left my portfolio on the table in his room. He smiled and said, "it's okay, we can get it after dinner." I wondered if this man thought that I possibly left it on purpose? Was that an honest smile he gave me, or was it a cunning smirk?

I gave him the benefit of the doubt because he had not proven to be that typical womanizing male. When we returned to his hotel room, I was pretty comfortable because we had a very professional and intellectual meeting that positioned me where he knew I was about my business. As we walked through the door, he began a conversation based on my earlier questions. The question was, "what do you think are some of your weaknesses in business?" His, in particular, was a weakness to intelligent, beautiful women. As soon as he made that comment, I could feel beads of sweat building up on my forehead. This is what I was trying to avoid the entire meeting. Why can't men just keep it professional?

I immediately thanked him for the interview, and I told him that it was time for me to leave. He then asked to see my portfolio. As much as I wanted to talk business, I responded, "well, maybe tomorrow at the office I can show you more. I promised my daughter we'd go trick or treating!" He stood up first and extended his hand to help me get off the couch. I thought he was a gentleman, but instead, he pulled me towards his lips! I instantly placed my hand between us, blocking his lips. He ended up kissing the back of my hand. "What the hell are you doing," I yelled and shoved him back. As if nothing ever happened, this man continued the conversation we were having before he violated my space. I was in absolute shock! He didn't acknowledge what he had just done but continued conversing as if I had just dreamt this whole thing up.

My legs were shaking. At this point, I was sweating bullets. I stood up, but my legs would not move. Getting to the door seemed like an eternity. As I was trying to open the door, Arnold came close behind me and began the conversation saying, "So you've never been with another man since your husband?" That's when I knew what had happened a few minutes earlier actually did happen. I slid away from the door, went over to the table, and grabbed my portfolio, but then my legs locked and all I could do was sit back down in the chair next to the desk. Now I was having trouble breathing. I needed an escape strategy fast.

In what seemed like minutes (which were actually seconds), I stood up with every bit of strength I could muster up, walked to the door, and opened it. Arnold asked me to wait for him to grab his coat from the room. I thought to myself, "foot help the body." When I finally got the door opened, I began speed walking down the hallway to the elevators. Shortly after, he came jogging up behind me. "Shoana, let me walk you to your car," he said. "It's fine, there is no need," I answered. He ignored my response and continued walking me to my car. The questions about infidelity continued. I got into my car, and he had the audacity to lean in for a hug. I slammed my door, started the ignition, hit reverse, and sped off down the street.   3 to 4 minutes into the drive, I pulled my car over and began to cry hysterically.

I felt so defeated. I can't tell my husband, parents, or even his wife about this because the question they will all ask is, "why did you go into his room if this was business?" I remember the trial of Kobe Bryant a few years ago. Most people blamed the girl for going to his room. That has stuck with me since. WHY DID I GO TO HIS ROOM? I am ashamed and disappointed because I know better. The only honest answer is that I thought it could benefit my growing business if I did whatever it took (within reason) to have him view my portfolio. I had never planned to meet in his room. Damn...If I tell anyone about this, they wouldn't believe that I would put myself in this situation as strong and calculated as I am. It's just plain desperate.

So now here I am, sitting on my bathroom floor with all my power snatched away from me. Was it worth my dignity?

PS: I will never put myself in this predicament ever again. My business will continue to grow with or without his investments. Why didn't I see this earlier? As women, our lives are worth so much more. I need to stop chasing the money. If I pursue my passion instead, the money will come.

I have nothing to show for it

It's all over! The recession is real, and I couldn't hold it together today as I moved the final pieces of furniture out of my beautiful studio. I locked the doors and walked away from my dream. I'm broken, and yeah, I do feel like a failure. The hardest part is letting go of my full-time staff and not giving them anything but one month's salary because I don't have anything to offer. I'm broke!

My accountant had warned me a couple of months ago that I should lay off some staff, but I guess I was in denial. I didn't believe that the recession would last for so long. My entire savings account has been wiped out by paying salaries and trying to make ends meet as the number of clients decreased daily. I just can't even pay my rent anymore, let alone staff. I have $1,000 in my savings account. The crazy thing is, my last year's tax return came in, and I had grossed almost $500,000, and here I am with $1,000 in my bank account.

One of the greatest lessons I've learned from this is to make sure I have something to show for everything I've ever made. I have a sexy blue classic Jaguar that I will probably have to sell along with our beautiful new home. I might even have to pawn my diamond, but just like that, I have nothing left after eight years of hard work. I don't even have money saved for college for my daughter.

This is completely distressing. How can my taxes show that I made all this money last year and only have $1,000 to my name? This is not the way to be successful. I don't want to go back to work for anyone. I need to reinvent myself and my business.

PS: God, give me one more chance to prove myself to you, and I promise I will never disappoint you again.

Reflection 3

As a child, we all want to hurry and grow up. We become exhausted and frustrated about waking up in the mornings to attend school. I remember saying multiple times during my last year in college that I couldn't wait to be an adult. If I knew then what I know now, I would take it back. Today, I would do anything to go back to the days when I didn't have so many bills and responsibilities. All I had to do was focus on my studies and allow my parents to handle all the other details about my life.

After college, I grew up pretty fast. Buying a house at 24 and starting a business with employees was a huge task to take on so young. I wanted to give up so many times, but something always reminded me that my dreams and goals were much more significant than that moment when things were not going well. Quitting was not an option. My conscience always reminded me to "power through it!"

Powering through obstacles is the only way I know. My life has not been a walk in the park. I've been hit with all types of curve balls but still I rise!

Marriage

MARRIAGE WOES

Marriage Woes

Most little girls dream about their wedding day. Perhaps they have a fantasy about their dream life with their incredible life partner and children. At least, that was what the thought of getting married meant to me. No one prepared me for the actual marriage experience. I don't think anyone could. After all, each experience can be beautifully unique, absolutely captivating, or devastatingly heartbreaking. Mine was.

Dude, we share a phone bill!

Today, my heart was shattered into a million pieces. Every woman knows when their home isn't right. There have been a few signs that something between him and I has not been right for months. Recently, he's been taking our baby out for drives claiming that he's putting her to sleep. At first, I thought it was a beautiful daddy and daughter bonding moment, but when I ask to join them from time to time, he is adamant that I stay home.

Whenever I call him while in the car, he's always rushing me off the phone, it always feels like he's on another call. After the phone call incident a few years ago, I never really regained trust in him. Honestly, it's probably because my heart knows something is not correct. My intuition never fails me.

This morning, I walked over to the mailbox to get the mail and found our phone bill. We usually don't even open the phone bill because we have a set amount that we pay monthly.

However, this month, it was much thicker than usual, so I opened it. We have had a joint phone bill since we got married. When I opened the bill, I noticed a number under his account from Minnesota. As I began to probe further, I noticed that this man calls this number up to eight times a day, EVERY DAY!!! He speaks to this person while driving to work, at lunchtime, during work hours, and on his drive home. What hurts the most is there are calls at 2 and 3 in the morning when I am asleep.

Naturally, I dialed the number, and sure enough, it was a female. "May I speak to Lisa," I asked. "I'm sorry you have the wrong number," she responded. That was enough for me to verify that it was a female with a hint of a Liberian accent. I hung up immediately, and out of nowhere, my emotions got the best of me. I felt like my tears could have filled an entire bucket.

My husband attends his regular guy sessions in Philly every Friday night. It's understood that Friday night is boy's night out, and I support that. I noticed on his bill that on Friday nights, when he leaves the house, there's one phone call made. There aren't any phone calls on his log the entire time he's out. Could it be possible that this girl lives here in Philly instead of Minnesota?

****

I could feel my pressure rising. My ears were hot, and sweat beads were dripping down my forehead. Rage had overcome me. Immediately, I grabbed my keys, jumped in the car, and headed to his office. I was furious and experiencing a mixture of unsettling emotions. I probably should not have been driving in that state, but I needed answers this morning.

I called his office line and asked him to meet me downstairs when I arrived.

He asked me what I was doing there, but I dismissed the questions and asked again, "meet me downstairs immediately!" He walked out of the building and got into the car. I quickly rolled up the windows and turned on the AC. I knew it would get ugly and didn't want bystanders to hear. I tried to talk, but I realized I couldn't even formulate words, so instead, I dropped the phone bill on his lap. "What is this," he asked? "It's our phone bill. Open it," I screamed. When he opened the bill, he noticed that I had highlighted every call made to the Minnesota number. "Whose number is that," I asked? He looked at this paper long and hard as if the numbers were mystically moving in circles on the sheet. This man had the nerve to look me in the face and ask, "What is this?" I asked the question again. "Whose number is this, and don't tell me you don't know because you certainly talk to this person every day, up to eight times a day, so clearly you know!" He was speechless, and then he said, " She's JUST my friend." I felt the tears welling up in my eyes. Before I knew it, I had broken out into the loudest, ugliest cry of my life. "I am neither stupid nor a child. I need you to get out of my car right now. When you get home this evening, the only thing I want to hear from you is the truth," I explained. Then I drove home to release it all on the pages of this journal.

PS: I think today might have changed my relationship with him forever.

It was planned.

I keep beating myself up for having these insane thoughts in my head. As women, we always talk about not letting a man take away our dignity or if a man cheats, we need to just leave and find a man who will treat us with respect. I know I am capable of surviving on my own but when a person is this deep in it, it's easier said than done.

There is so much to think about, like how much time and energy I have invested in this man and this marriage. Letting go of it means that these chics win. It means that I'm not trusting God and living up to my vows by dealing with the good and bad of marriage. I'll be honest, I wasn't ready for the lies, deceit, and disrespect that entered my marriage.

I hate to admit this, but I still want another child and want it with him. When I got married, it was forever. My parents have been married for over 30 years. As a little girl, I always dreamt about being married to the same man forever with two or three children and raising them in a Christian home. Am I being naïve to think that this can still be fixed? My grandmother has always said, "where there's a will, there's a way," and I know that God can fix this. I've always wanted my children to have the same last name. I don't want to be that mom with each of my children having different fathers. It's just not the Christian way and certainly not for me. I must be losing it because I've wanted to get pregnant during this war between my husband and me for a year now. The relationship has become toxic and barely intimate. He knows I want a baby, and maybe secretly, I think this baby will fix the brokenness in our relationship.

****

Guess what? I found out that I am pregnant today! I thought I would be excited. Unfortunately, I'm actually really numb. If our relationship continues with this level of stress, I might lose my baby. Honestly, making a sacrifice like this is for my daughter who's been begging for a sibling; someone to play with; someone to love her; someone to sit with her when mommy's crying or mommy's sad. Is it selfish of me to desire a child even though I know that this marriage won't work or is it what I need to get through the separation that's about to happen? I just don't know. I'm so confused and broken tonight. I can't really talk to anybody about this ridiculous idea for fear that folks might try to talk me out of it.

I'm a communicator who can't communicate with anyone at this time. I'm ashamed of what's happening in my home. I'm ashamed of not being that person everyone thinks I am. I'm ashamed of being weak and letting a man manipulate me to the point where I'm staying with him, knowing that he's cheated on me multiple times. I need to do better; I need to be better, but I just don't know how.

Not in front of our daughter.

The rage has got to stop!!! I don't think I can do this anymore. I've been in a relationship where I have allowed my husband to cheat, and I have stayed because I want my daughter to grow up with a father figure in the home. Am I crazy? When I was younger, I remember thinking that the first guy who cheats on me would get his walking papers, but it's not until you get into a deep relationship with someone and invest time, and emotions, and have a child with them that you feel truly stuck. I now understand why a woman stays in a toxic and unhealthy relationship. I realize that love has made me stupid or is it enough to say the main reason I'm staying is because of my daughter's beautiful relationship with her father? I've tried everything that I could to keep her stable, but I realize I'm hurting her more than helping her today.

In the middle of a huge yelling match with her father, our little girl stood right between the two of us with her hands to her ears, shouting as loud as she could shout the words "la la la la la la" until we finally stopped and paid attention. Our little girl was crying out for help. She wanted us to stop yelling but was too scared to use her words. My baby was suffering greater than both of us, and she didn't deserve it.

After today, there will no longer be arguments in front of my child with any man. I realized today this marriage is ending. This is over! I've decided that I'm going to leave today, and I'm taking my daughter. We're going to my parents. What happens next... I'm not sure. I've hidden this from my entire family for years. I guess I never wanted to be judged. My child doesn't deserve this, and I don't deserve this. Clearly, I've lost myself! I don't know what happened to the strong, vibrant, and bold woman in me. I've got to find her again. She's lost and allowed herself to stay in this toxic relationship that has hurt her and hurt her child significantly. What kind of woman would do this to her child? Me!

Moving backwards

I don't know why but I've decided to move back home with him. Maybe it's because I feel incomplete, and perhaps I want to give this marriage everything I've got. I think it might mainly be because I feel like if God asked me today if I did everything to save my marriage, my answer would be no. I need it to be yes, so I'm trying again. I guess another reason is that I'm four months pregnant now.

I saw the light

I woke up at around 6 a.m. to go to the bathroom yesterday morning. After wiping myself, I noticed blood on the tissue. I am 4 months pregnant and blood at four months is not a good sign. I woke my husband up and told him that I was bleeding. "Call the hospital," he suggested. I called my midwife, and she told me what I was not prepared to hear. "You are most likely having a miscarriage, and there is nothing you can do right now but wait," she instructed. She asked me just to monitor the bleeding. I couldn't go back to sleep. I laid awake in bed thinking about how this was all my fault. If I had stopped fighting with my husband, if I had just stopped stressing and stayed healthy and focused on the little soul in my belly, all would have been well. I just returned home two nights ago after leaving my home to escape my husband and this toxic relationship. Now, this!

I had an urge to go back to the bathroom, so I did, but nothing but blood came out this time. It was happening. I was losing the one thing that I knew could possibly keep my marriage together. I was losing the new baby that I wanted more than anything in this world. Amid my mental breakdown on the toilet, something very wrong happened. I felt an object the size of what felt like a giant orange slowly ease its way out of my vagina. When I realized it was my fetus, I tried desperately to keep it in but failed. I heard a large splash in the toilet. I'm unsure what possessed me, but I immediately flushed the toilet. In mid-flush, I snapped and wanted my baby back. My body went limp, and I fell to the floor, and wrapped my arms around the base of the toilet, pleading with it to send my baby back. What if it was still alive? What if the doctors could save her/him? What have I done? I was now sitting in a pool of blood. I screamed for my husband at the top of my lungs. He came running into the bathroom, and I told him to call the doctor.

Before I knew it, I was lying on my back on the floor. I figured I had fainted because I saw my husband and daughter standing over me in horror when I opened my eyes. "Wake up! Wake up, mommy! Don't die," Monahdee screamed. I could feel sweat dripping all over my body. It was hot, so I asked them to turn on the air conditioner. It's interesting what fear can do to a person. My husband couldn't figure out how to turn it on even though he turns it on daily. Meanwhile, my daughter was fanning me with a magazine and yelling, "Mommy, don't die!" I promised her that I wouldn't die as I asked my husband to call the ambulance quickly.

As he tried to help me up, I blacked out again for the second time. By the time the ambulance arrived, I had already fainted four times. I had lost so much blood that I could barely sit up. They rushed me to the hospital, and I was lying in this hospital room for hours. I was bleeding so much that my sister and mother had to change my sheets several times. There were not enough doctors on call. With every cramped came excruciating pain. I knew at that moment that I was dying. I was ok with that, considering I felt like I deserved to die after having a miscarriage because I chose to continuously live in a high-stress environment. I had a choice to walk away from this toxic relationship and get my life together. After all, God had blessed me with the pregnancy I wanted. Why didn't I just leave to protect my babies?

I sent my daughter with daddy out of my emergency room to the waiting room and told my mom and sister that I loved them and needed to rest. When I closed my eyes, there was a sense of peace. I noticed a bright light that felt so warm and comforting. Now, as I reflect on that moment yesterday, I believe that light was leading to the gates to heaven. It's tough to verbalize, but I felt like I was being called. I heard a faint sound in the background that sounded like a machine that had flatlined. I didn't feel myself leaving my body like in the movies, but I could hear all the doctors saying my name and asking me repeatedly to open my eyes. I thought I had to open them, but I chose not to because it was more peaceful and pleasant with my eyes closed. Their voices were getting faint. I heard my mom frantically saying, "Shoana, you can't die. Your Monahdee needs you." Those words triggered something in me that restarted my body. I quickly opened my eyes to assure her that I was okay and the constant tone of the machine turned into a series of short beeps. That's when it hit me. God offered me a choice yesterday. He showed me the easy way out. I didn't follow the light but decided to stay and be a mother to my daughter, and for whatever that meant, I found so much strength in my faith. I promised God that my situation was going to change. I was reborn. I lost my second child, but I gained a second chance at life.

Who did I marry?

I'm not even sure how to start this journal entry. I am absolutely out of words at this moment. So allow me to begin with the back story. Earlier this year, we moved out of our home to an apartment in Delaware. We had decided to finally relocate to Liberia. Before moving, I forwarded my mail to our new place in downtown Wilmington, DE. The bills related to my work were forwarded to my office mailbox in Brookhaven, PA. It is customary that when I get home from work, I grab the mail from our mailbox before entering the elevator and heading to my apartment on the 5th floor. Lately, I've noticed that my husband has been getting to the box before me. I didn't think anything of it since he would leave my mail on the table.

Today, I drove into the parking lot at my office, pulled up by the mailboxes, and grabbed a stack of envelopes. The envelope on the top was from Home Depot, a hardware store I had not shopped at for months. "Why are they sending me a bill," I thought. Little did I know that in that envelope was a bill for over $1400. It stated that I had bought a good amount of lawn care equipment from their store. As soon as I got to my desk, I immediately began to dial their customer service line. When the phone started to ring, it occurred that this might not be an error. My husband and I had had several disagreements about him investing our money in a lawn care business in Liberia. I didn't want to kill his dreams of being an entrepreneur in Liberia, but I also knew that in order to have a successful business venture, he would have to do some market research. Either way, he didn't take my advice. Instead, he took my store card and used my credit without my knowledge. In other words, he stole from me.

Now it all made sense. He was intercepting the mail at home, hoping to get to the bill before me. He had no idea that the bill would come directly to me at work. I really serve an awesome God.

But wait....So was he going to leave the country without paying this bill? He was getting ready to leave for Liberia and had no income coming in. How dare he do this to me. I'm so exhausted from these daily arguments. Is he that desperate that he would steal my card to make his dreams a reality while not even worrying about the consequences of me finding out?

Now I'm having severe trust issues. Clearly, he is out of cash and preparing to leave in a few days. However, I have noticed a few new purchases. Where is this money coming from? Our joint account is empty because I made sure to take out what was left of my money a few months back. The only thing we had left was our daughter's account, but I'm sure he wouldn't use that...or would he? Just as the thought occurred, I grabbed my car keys abruptly, jumped in my car, and headed to my credit union, where we had opened an account for our daughter earlier that year.

I could feel my pressure rise as I swerved past cars on the highway. The credit union was about 20 mins away from our apartment in Delaware. I began to think about what I would do if I found out that he had taken the money out of her account too. "I'm definitely calling the police," I shouted out loud in the car.

As soon as I walked up to the teller, she saw the look of distress on my face. We knew each other on a first-name basis. "Hey Shoana, are you ok," she began. "I'm good, Trina. Just a bit tired today."
I was nervous even to ask her the question. Before finding the words, she stated, "So, do you have the authorization forms I gave your husband yesterday?" What was she talking about? "The forms," I asked? "Yes," she replied. "Your husband came by yesterday to close your daughter's account, but since you both opened the account, you need to sign the form as well. I felt my knees get weak immediately. I had to hold on to the counter and take a deep breath. She could tell something was not right based on the look on my face. "Can I talk to you privately, I asked?" There was a line behind me, and

I could feel myself about to cry. She quickly closed her counter and asked the teller next to her to care for her line.

As soon as we stepped into an enclosed glass cubicle, my tears became unstoppable. She grabbed a box of tissues and offered them to me. "I'm so sorry," I began. I explained that my husband had violated my trust and begged her to flag the account if he came back. I'm not sure if he wanted to use the money for himself or make sure I could not access It. Either way, the money was still there, and I had complete control of it.

As I exited the bank today, I wasn't sure who I was married to anymore. I am crushed...

The audacity

I've been trying to write since my husband left a few days ago to head back to Liberia, but I've been in utter shock.

Monahdee had been struggling since her dad left for Liberia in December 2008. We had made a joint decision to relocate our family after an earlier visit to Liberia right after the war back in 2005. The plan was that he would leave in December, and we would follow in June so that Monahdee could finish 1st grade.

After my miscarriage in September this past year, I realized that perhaps this move was not the best decision at this time in our life. We needed to strengthen our marriage, and figure out a way to keep our family together. Distance is the last thing we need. A month before he left in December, I brought up the idea of him staying for a few more months so that we could rebuild our relationship. I was still mourning the loss of our unborn child. He was entirely against the idea. "Let's stick to the plan," he stated. It felt as if something was pulling him to Liberia, and nothing would stop his plans. I knew that it would be the end of our marriage if he left.

The original plan was that he would arrive six months earlier to get settled with work and find a place for us to stay when we got to Liberia. However, after about four months on the continent, Monahdee began to struggle. She's been missing her father so much. She even misses her unborn baby sister/brother that I miscarried.

*****

A few weeks ago, I received a call from her teacher requesting a conference. Ms. Anette stated that Monahdee was making up stories about her baby sister, but Anette was aware that she was an only child. We figured out she was suffering from the trauma of losing the baby, and her father leaving the country was the cause of her actions. After talking with Ms. Anette, I immediately called him up and asked him to come home to visit for just two weeks. He claimed that a two-week visit would be tough financially, and he didn't have the money. I was apprehensive about offering to pay because I didn't like what had unfolded right before he left in December. My daughter's mental health is way more important to me, so I bought the ticket, and he agreed to come.

We were so excited to see him. I kept thinking that the separation would make our hearts grow fonder for each other, and it would help our marriage, so I planned a getaway for the three of us. I got a two-bedroom condo out on a lake. It was perfect. Monahdee had her own room, and we had the other room. I remember that night so clearly. I had put Monahdee to bed and walked into our bedroom. I'd hoped for one of the most amazing, wonderfully intimate nights with my husband. It was a beautiful evening, but I will never forget how long he lasted in bed. I've been married for several years now, and I know my husband as well as I know myself. We hadn't touched each other for four months, so when we got in bed, I expected he would cum pretty fast. However, this man lasted for over 25 freaking minutes. This revealed that not only had he recently had sex but that he was constantly having it to have such a prolonged erection. I felt completely numb, and my body shut down. Tears slowly filled my eyes as he finally orgasmed in me. What was I thinking? How could I possibly have thought that this would work?

*****

We always use condoms, so before that night, we had stopped by the convenience store for a box of Trojans. During his stay, we used three out of the pack of 12. After he left, there were only three remaining in the box. He had the audacity to take an extra six condoms out of the box and leave me with a half-empty box as if I wouldn't notice or calculate. I addressed him about the six missing condoms, and he responded, "Perhaps your dad used them." He was not only arrogant but highly disrespectful.

I knew that if I'd asked him if he had been cheating on me, his response would be no, so I used a bit of reverse psychology.
"My dear," I started. "I honestly know that we've been apart for a long time, and I know that you as a man have needs. I just have to say that I'm so proud of you for using condoms. I want you to know that I totally understand." His response was a lip dropper. He responded, "I must be the luckiest man in the world to have a wife as understanding as you." This fool had just been played, and he had no idea. All I wanted was confirmation, and his statement was ENOUGH! I also confirmed that I wasn't going crazy and that he was cheating. Those words sealed the deal. How could he possibly think that I would be okay with infidelity? Was he crazy?

Unwelcome home

It's been one month since Monahdee and I joined my husband in Liberia. I have not been able to journal because you could not possibly begin to believe what my life has now come to.

The plan was that my husband would come to Liberia 6 months ahead to secure a stable job and a place we could call home. A month before I arrived, we agreed that he would look for a suitable place for us to live that included electricity and running water. That plan had not materialized. He had so many excuses instead of solutions. I made one phone call to a family friend, secured housing, and negotiated a rate for us. All he had to do was take our barrels full of our home furnishings (we had shipped in advance) and set up our new home. Do you think he did that?

We arrived in Liberia on my 33rd birthday. I was fully aware at this point that my marriage was practically over. Moving to Liberia would be a new start for me. I planned to hire a driver and a nanny! Both of which I would not be able to afford if I stayed in the US. I'm an entrepreneur. I just need a few months to get on my feet, and I will be able to sustain my daughter and myself.

When he opened the door of the home I had rented for us; absolutely nothing was done. He had dropped the barrels off, and that was it. No dusting, cleaning, not even sheets were on the beds. There wasn't even water in the fridge. He did stop to buy toilet paper and bread from a street vendor on the drive home. I was furious! How could his wife and daughter travel thousands of miles and come home to four empty walls and barrels in the middle of the floor? It was my birthday, and I did everything to hold back the tears. "Where are the sheets," I exclaimed. "They are at the apartment," he answered. The apartment was the basement of his mother's house and where he had resided for the last six months. When he was moving back in December, I had come with him to decorate the apartment and make it feel like home. Even after the whole ordeal with him stealing my store card, I still bought him a bed, living room furniture, and even wall hangings. I guess I wanted him to appreciate the effort and put forth more effort towards saving our marriage.

I stayed up half the night regretting coming to join him in Liberia. What did I actually expect? Why did I need this marriage to work so badly? Am I so worried about what others will think, or am I secretly obsessed with him! What the hell!

The Nerve

My husband had the audacity to give his side chick housing in our Apartment. The day after we arrived, I asked him to take me early in the morning to the apartment, so I could get our sheets for the bed. "You want to go this early," he hesitated. I confirmed, and we all got into his big red Ford pickup and headed to the apartment.

A middle-aged dark-skin woman opened the door. He quickly introduced her as Patricia, his friend from America who was working on a job assignment and needed a place to stay while the construction of her home was completed. I smiled and greeted her. She hit me with the "smile and look away." I know that all too well from the numerous other women that had affairs with my husband. I didn't say another word. I went into the guest room and started collecting items to take with us. I could see her clearly in the next room, pretending to be on her phone. She was noticeably nervous. This trick had the nerve to stay in the house while I was present. I got this! I put on a show for her.

My husband was by my side, helping me look through the barrels, and I intentionally began to flirt with him as if we had just met. I made it a point to be loud so she would hear every word. Sure enough, she stood up and walked out of the apartment. "That's confirmed," I thought to myself!
A few days later, I went back to the apartment while she was at work. My husband had hired a man that had worked for my family to wash and clean for her. Does he not know about loyalty? This man was loyal to my family and not to him and his girlfriend. I convinced the man that I already knew what was happening, and he revealed the entire story as if he just had to get it off his chest. Exactly like I thought, They had been living together in that same apartment. So I was right; my husband was getting ample sex daily. But to have her

stay in our apartment after I got here was insulting.

I managed to find her number on his phone and politely sent her a text stating that since I was a woman of God, I gave her 30 days to find a place to live. I also included that she was not the first, second, third, fourth, or last woman that my husband had cheated with. I concluded by telling her to focus on working on her own marriage since she left her husband in the States to come and chase after a married man. She then proceeded to report the message to my husband. He called me to inquire about my text to Patricia and that she didn't have to move out. After all, it was not my place to tell his friend that she had to move out of his Mother's home.

That was it!!! His words were the final straw.

Welcoming Sarafina

Amid all the heartache, finally a bit of sunshine. I talked about adopting a child from Liberia for the past two years now. Initially, my husband was skeptical, but after I lost my baby, he was surprisingly supportive of the idea. For me, adoption was a way to give back. God has blessed my life, and I want to pay it forward and bless others.

****

A few days before I arrived in Liberia, my husband called and shared a story about Anthony, a man in Maryland County who experienced his wife's tragic death. She was brutally murdered while traveling to Sierra Leone to purchase goods to sell. The story was all over the radio. Anthony shared with the press that he needed help. He was unable to take care of their eight children because his wife was the family's breadwinner.

My Sister-in-law worked in Plebo, Maryland, where they lived and knew the family. She wanted to help, so she immediately called my husband. A while back, he had mentioned to her that I wanted to adopt a child from Liberia so Monahdee would have a sibling and playmate. Unfortunately, this was the worst timing considering our troubled marriage. I tried to back out of it, but it was too late. He had already told his sister that we would take the youngest of the eight children, and she would be arriving soon. My emotions were all over the place. My marriage was about to end, and now we are about to adopt a child? How was this going to work? I learned a while ago not to question God, so I said a prayer and gave it all to him.

****

We stood at Spriggs Payne Airport earlier today, anxiously waiting for the UN flight that would arrive with our new daughter. We knew nothing about her, not even her name. When the flight landed, the doors opened and a few people walked down the steps. A beautiful, chubby little girl stepped out of the airplane door. She looked about four years old. She was wearing a green shirt, a striped skirt, and black dress shoes. A can of coke and a pack of crackers were in her little hands. She looked like she had been crying. I ran to the lady holding her hand and thanked her for accompanying my daughter. We introduced ourselves and asked her for her name. "My name, Big ma," she responded. She was adorable. I hugged her so tight that she physically had to push me away. Poor child, she had no idea why I had been crying. So much was going through my mind at that moment. There were tears of both joy and pain simultaneously. I quickly composed myself, and we started the journey home, where Monahdee had been patiently waiting.

As soon as we pulled into the yard, Monahdee and her nanny were standing on the porch. She came running to the car when we parked. I opened the door and stepped out of the backseat with her new sister. Monahdee asked for her name, and I responded, "her name is Big Ma." We asked Big Ma if she wanted Monahdee to give her a new name, and she responded with an excited yes. We quickly turned to Monahdee and asked what she wanted to call Big Ma, and she said, "Sarafina!" Big Ma repeated the name a few times. When asked if she liked it, she said, "I like Sarafina!"

The girls spent the rest of the evening staring at each other and barely talking. I could only imagine what was going through both of their heads. This was so new for all of us. I was just grateful Monahdee could focus her time on getting to know her sister instead of watching me cry. I've been in such a dark place these days. I'm really not sure how to navigate through all the changes in my life.

PS: God, I need you more than ever now.

I'm done but not before I take what's mine.

Today I just did the unthinkable. I reclaimed my power, and I feel great!

This morning I walked into my husband's office and asked for his keys to the Ford truck. I traded keys with him. I told him I needed to move a few things. We were not speaking at this point in our relationship, so he didn't ask me for details. I asked my driver to find a few strong men on the street. "We are moving a lot of furniture this morning," I joked.

We found three guys, put them in the back of the pickup, and headed to the apartment. The cleaner was there cleaning. I walked in and began collecting every single item I had bought. Even the wall hangings were thrown in the truck. Ironically, after I was done, the apartment resembled my empty apartment on the day I first arrived. All her things were placed on the floor. I was proud of myself for not destroying any of it. The only thing

I didn't take was the bed because I wanted her to at least have a soft spot to sleep. Although she didn't deserve to be given any grace, I just felt better about not leaving her on the cold floor!

My phone rang at about 6 pm. It was my soon to be ex-husband on the line asking me if I had cleared out the apartment. "Are you asking me why I took everything I owned from our apartment?" I asked. "Well, I purchased all of those items for us to enjoy, not your side, chick!Why would I furnish an apartment for your other woman?" I politely hung up the phone, grabbed a sheet of paper, pen, and began drafting my final letter to him.

It's time for a new start

It was the perfect evening. The wind from the ocean was refreshing. I had made dinner reservations at RLJ Beach Resort with my husband. It was about a 20-minute drive from where we lived. Today felt like a prayer was answered. We were having a rare but much-needed stress-free day. While Monahdee and Sarafina stayed at home with the nanny, just the two of us sat at a table near the window overlooking the pool.

I had tucked the letter deep into my back pocket. The night before, I decided I would write my final love letter. I kept feeling for it throughout the night to make sure it was still there. I poured my heart into it and carefully crafted every word, so I had to make sure it didn't drop out of my pocket.

Dinner was delicious. We laughed, smiled, and even joked a little. I pretended we were on the best date of our lives. It made what was about to happen a bit easier. Through the evening, I believe that he might have been thinking that I was accepting his double life and choosing to stay. He looked so happy and relieved.

After dinner, I grabbed his hand and asked for a stroll on the beach at sunset. We watched the sunset gently disappear on the horizon. Romance was in the air. He softly pulled me in for a kiss, and for the first time, I felt nothing. No connection, no longing, no subconscious feeling of love and yearning. Just emptiness...complete emptiness. I allowed him to kiss me. Perhaps that would trigger something. NOPE...nothing. I gently pulled the letter out of my back pocket while continuing the kiss. Once our lips parted, I opened the letter, asked him to allow me to complete it before he spoke, then began to reclaim my power with each word I read out loud.

Reflection 4

Cheater list

My marriage is over. He has moved out and I am moving on...

Today, I'm making a list of all the things I've noticed over the years regarding cheating. I'll be sure to use it to advise a few friends in the future.

Your partner might be cheating:

* If your partner takes their phone every place they go, including the restroom… beware!

* If your partner always places their phone face down, they might be hiding something from you.

* If you ask them for the time or just to look at their phone, and your partner takes it from you immediately afterward.

* If every time you call your partner when they are out, they give you a reason they need to call you back…red flag!

* If your partner tells you every Friday or Saturday night is boys/girls night. It's their way of telling you never to expect to be invited. Just know that there's a possibility that they are not just hanging with the crew.

* If your partner received a text or a phone call and can't respond or take the call in front of you.

* If your partner repeatedly comes home after midnight and blames it on work.

* If your partner tells you that they are helping a friend in need repeatedly, and you have never heard of this friend before.

- If you keep seeing a particular person's name in your partner's phone log and they never mentioned that friend to you. It's probably a side thing.

- If you go out and your partner introduces you to a friend that completely avoids eye contact with you.

- If you go to a gathering with your partner and their friends are looking at you in shock or acting overly nice to you. They might be feeling sorry for you because they know what your partner has been up to.

- If your partner never mentions a name but repeatedly refers to the same person as "my workmate/coworker" instead of their real name.

- If your partner ever makes a mistake and calls you by a different name. It basically means they have been spending a lot of time with another person.

To be continued...